WORD

M000105363

"At the Ronald McDonald House Away From Home for families with children experiencing critical illnesses. These families are in the crosshairs of crisis each day—and so is our team. *After the Shock: Getting You Back On The Road To Resilience When Crisis Hits You Head On* is a salve for wounded spirits and emotions, no matter the source. The clarity with which the reader is taken through comfort, control, community, and connection sets a wonderful foundation that leads to healing through learning from our life experiences, building on correct assumptions, and reaching out to the proper resources around us. This is more than a book; it is like being with a great friend. It will be of immense comfort to both our guest families and our team."

> —Oie Osterkamp, MBA, executive director, Ronald McDonald
> House of Durham

"Written in a conversational style with stories to illustrate key points, *After the Shock* reduces the confusion of crisis by providing practical tools for those going through a tough time."

> —Mary Cantando, founder, The Woman's Advantage®

"*After the Shock* is a tremendous resource for people facing unbearable realities in life. It helps a person forge a new path forward in an authentic way. Healing is not easy, but Becky Sansbury's book has warm, wise, and witty wisdom for people who know life can be better and are willing to explore what they can do. I highly recommend this book as a personal reference and as a book to share with friends who are facing a dark night of the soul."

> —Allegra Jordan, MBA, managing director, Innovation Abbey,
> best-selling author of *Harvard 1914* and *The End of Innocence*

"*After the Shock* is an excellent book for those in the military who need support during inflection points. I highly recommend *After the Shock.*"

> —Curtis D. Strong, MS, MEd, Chief Warrant Officer (Retired),
> United States Army, Special Operations Command

Deep uncertainty escorts crisis. Reach for *After the Shock* to benefit from a wisdom that gently nurtures healing. Sansbury reminds us of the power within ourselves and our communities to replace loss with resilience. Resilience, it turns out, is a well-coordinated enterprise. Brava to Sansbury for shedding light on the confusion of shock and revealing the path forward.

> —Lee Anne McClymont, MHA, host and producer,
> Courage Cocktail Radio Show, WCOM FM 103.5

Becky Sansbury

After *the*
SHOCK

Getting You Back On The
ROAD TO RESILIENCE
When Crisis Hits You Head On

Copyright © 2015 Becky Sansbury
All rights reserved. Except for brief quotations in articles or reviews, no part
of this book may be reproduced in any manner without prior written
permission from the publisher.

Published by Real Life Communication, Raleigh, North Carolina
Visit www.beckysansbury.com

Printed in the United States of America

To purchase quantities in bulk, contact the publisher directly at
becky@beckysansbury.com.

ISBN 978-0-692-44757-4

This book is dedicated to my patients, families, and colleagues at Hospice of Wake County (now Transitions LifeCare), my clients and colleagues at Avadon Group, and my parents, all of whom demonstrated resilience in action.

TABLE OF CONTENTS

Introduction

Shock became reality when I was twenty-seven years old. During what was supposed to be a standard pregnancy checkup, I learned that the baby inside me had died, but I had not miscarried. Suddenly a time of great anticipation turned to a time of great sorrow. The sorrow deepened when I learned I would need to carry the unborn child for another month to increase the chance of a successful pregnancy in the future. Reality intensified when a year later I had to repeat this experience. Another year later, I suffered a third pregnancy loss, though this time it was a traditional miscarriage.

We closed the nursery door. Tired of tears, anxiety, and a gut-wrenching roller coaster of emotions, we couldn't even look at that room.

Lest it sound like my life was one long pregnancy drama, I am happy to report eventually I was able to bear two healthy children. The nursery did finally become a happy place.

What was obvious to me was that I did not know how to manage the shock of those miscarriages—and the many well-intentioned people around me did not know how to either. Oprah wasn't yet interviewing experts on such life situations, and there didn't seem to be any way to learn in practical points what to do. So my husband and I muddled through. Casseroles and cards, hugs without words, and caring friends and family helped us heal.

Fortunately our marriage grew stronger with our unified quest to parent a child. But within five years our marriage would be tested again when my young husband suffered a stroke and related emotional challenges. Once again well-meaning friends offered what they could, but admitted they didn't really know what to do or say. The next three years showed clearly that this time the marriage would not last. Not only was my heart broken, but three years of medical, financial, and emotional uncertainty left me in a perpetual state of chaos. I yearned for the slightly boring, normal life I had taken for granted.

Now a single mother in my mid-thirties with two young daughters, I returned to school to embark upon a new career. I entered seminary with the clear intent of becoming a chaplain, but only a modest plan of how to get there. I leaned heavily on friends and family during this time (what would I have done without my parents?), and my resilience grew through them as well as through the help of wise professionals in my field.

After seminary, I trained as a clinical chaplain (one who works in a medical setting). This education helped explain in retrospect the process I had gone through with my miscarriages and my husband's stroke. It helped me understand my insomnia, weight loss, self-blame, and fractured relationship with God (in spite of my sense of professional calling). Similarly, it helped me forgive the people who promised to help, but "disappeared," and emulate the people who showed up consistently, even during emotional times.

I gained the insight that ordinary people can make their way through unimaginable challenges. Even when you know the circumstances are tough, you don't always realize how extraordinary they are. Sometimes when I relate my story, I see on the other person's face a shocked look of "Oh my goodness," and I'm reminded how much I've been through.

During my chaplain residency, I began to truly listen to other people's stories, and I became intrigued with resilience in the face of extreme circumstance. I knew this form of resilience didn't require advanced degrees or the kind of clinical training I was privileged to receive, but I hadn't yet figured out what it was that helped people move from that initial crisis reaction toward stability and resilience.

In month eleven of my twelve-month chaplain residency, I still didn't have a job lined up. My daughters loved going to school in Raleigh, and we wanted to stay put, but I had no idea how I was going to make that happen. One day at the hospital, I ran into a buddy who mentioned an opening for a chaplain in Raleigh at Hospice of Wake County. I didn't want to admit to him that I had no idea what "hospice" was; in 1989 few people did.

While we sometimes attach great significance to a surprising event ("It was my destiny"), my situation was more like an arranged marriage. They needed a chaplain quickly; I needed a job quickly. I'm happy to say we fell in love along the way and were together for almost fourteen years. Not only did I enjoy my defined position, I discovered a special connection to the entire field of end-of-life work. That led to a national community of colleagues who consistently supported each other.

As a hospice chaplain, I spent my time with patients who had life-limiting (also known as "terminal") illnesses and were expected to live six months or less. In reality I probably spent more time with the patients' families and close friends. While I was there to provide comfort and counsel to *them*, all these people became *my* teachers in the lessons of life. At a time you might expect people to be barely surviving, I saw many people flourishing. Again I wondered, how did they do it?

I began to notice patterns in things said to me. I began to hear common concerns. "I don't want to hurt." "I don't want to be afraid." "I don't want be alone, but I don't want to be a burden to my family and friends." "I don't want to feel like all of this is pointless." I heard these statements over and over. Sometimes the words were different, but the themes were always the same.

After I left hospice and following a few years as a family caregiver, I joined Avadon Group, a team specializing in career transition during the height of the recent recession. This is where I realized the principles I'd begun to recognize in hospice care were applicable to any form of life disruption.

The Four Cs we'll cover in this book (Comfort, Control, Community, and Connection) began to emerge from those statements made years ago by hospice patients and reiterated by people in multiple areas of crisis and disruption. These Four Cs are the foundation of our life's stability. They come into play throughout our lives, but particularly in times of crisis.

But I knew the Four Cs themselves were not enough. While they identified fundamental human conditions that could provide stability, there was something else needed during crisis or disruption. I needed to find a process for moving from the initial reaction to a shock, back to stability, and then on to resilience.

During a time of personal and professional upheaval in my own life, I hired a coach. I was in the midst of a second divorce, and I didn't have a job. But I had one treasure: over the years many people had handed me gems of insight and understanding about moving through crisis. I just needed a way to translate that insight to other people. I needed a way to get that message out.

My coach helped me articulate what was rolling around in my head and distill it into a process, E-A-R: first understanding our Experience and that of others, then naming and testing our Assumptions, and finally assessing the Resources we have and need.

My assumption is that you are reading this book to get back on the road to resilience as you work through a crisis or to become more effective as you help someone else through a crisis. I still don't have all the answers, but I want to share what I've learned along the way. You will fill in some of your own answers—and maybe raise a few more questions.

WHAT TO EXPECT FROM THIS BOOK

As you'll read shortly, one of the key characteristics of someone in crisis is difficulty concentrating and absorbing complex information. With that in mind, I've designed this book to be easily digestible and its advice simple and practical.

The next chapter offers the lay of the land with a description of crisis and resilience, plus a preview of the terrain we'll be covering in the *After the Shock*™ model.

In the rest of the book you'll find:

* A large dose of stories, analogies, and examples to illustrate the concepts we cover, with an anchor story at the beginning of each chapter and a highlight story to close each chapter
* Tools such as checklists, suggestions, charts, and questions for reflection
* White space in each chapter for taking notes and answering reflection questions
* A summary at the end of each chapter that recaps key points for easy reference
* A detailed table of contents at the back of the book for easily locating key concepts
* A compilation of the chapter summaries at the back of the book for easy reference
* Notes and references for each chapter at the back of the book

Living in North Carolina, I became a big fan of Kay Yow, beloved basketball coach at NC State University. One of the winningest coaches in NCAA history, Yow died in 2009 after twice fighting breast cancer. One of her famous quotes was "Don't wallow in self-pity; swish your feet and get out." My version of that is "It's OK to *not* be OK for a while; you just don't want to stay that way."

This book gives you a sustainable process so when you're hit with a crisis you can move from a place of reaction—and perhaps some warranted toe-swishing—to stability and ultimately on toward resilience.

Overview: Getting the Lay of the Land

There cannot be a crisis next week. My schedule is already full.
—Henry A. Kissinger

Life is extraordinarily resilient. It's been around for over a billion years.
—Geoffrey West, British scientist and TED speaker

WHAT DO WE MEAN BY *CRISIS*?

When you hear the word *crisis*, what do you think? A dramatic car wreck. A critical medical diagnosis. The announcement of a divorce. Job loss. Natural disaster. Death. Certainly each one of those qualifies as a major life shock. And let's not overlook the mini-shocks within those crises or the smaller events that disrupt our lives more frequently. A fender bender in morning rush-hour traffic. Personal information getting hacked. An uncomfortable but not life-threatening illness. Being overlooked for a promotion.

Merriam-Webster offers a basic definition of *crisis*: "a difficult or dangerous situation that needs serious attention." It also offers a more robust one: "an unstable or crucial time or state of affairs in which a decisive change is impending; *especially* one with the distinct possibility of a highly undesirable outcome." (Notice the word "unstable" in the second definition. One of my main goals is to help you regain stability during and after a crisis.)

Whether large or small, a crisis causes disruption and de-stabilization, sometimes for a brief burst, sometimes indefinitely. The terms *chronic* and *acute* are traditional descriptors of illness and crisis, but it's important to acknowledge that smaller crises, let's call them *difficulties*, are still crises. There are also some *life-altering* crises that go well beyond the traditional definition of chronic.

Figure 1 lays out these different types of crises by length of impact and the degree of disruption.

Figure 1 Types of Crisis

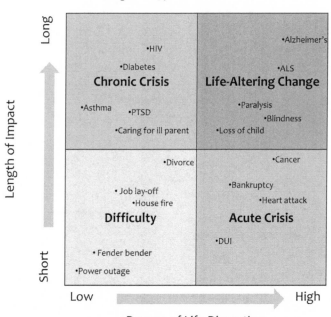

Difficulty – The mildest form of crisis is still a crisis. A fender bender. A short-term job loss. A kitchen fire. A basement flood. Certainly these types of events can be more dramatic than the mild term "difficulty" might suggest, but many of life's crises are ultimately manageable and we move on quickly.

Acute Crisis – Merriam-Webster defines *acute* as "having a sudden onset, sharp rise, and short course" or "lasting a short time." A car accident with injuries. A heart attack. Something happens; you address it. The severity is greater than that of a difficulty, and there may be some longer-term implications (you may have to eat better and exercise more after a heart attack), but the situation basically gets resolved (the heart attack itself does not last for months).

Chronic Crisis – Merriam-Webster defines *chronic* as "marked by long duration or frequent recurrence; not acute." Think of ongoing diseases such as asthma or diabetes. They never go away, but may be well managed on a daily basis (fairly low disruption), possibly with periodic flare-ups requiring a trip to the ER. Or think of chronic unemployment, typically defined as six to twelve months or more, which we saw in the most recent recession.

Life-Altering Change – The opposite quadrant from *difficulty* is *life-altering change*. High disruption *and* long-term impact. Something dramatic happens that requires a complete realignment of how we live. Losing a limb. Having a stroke and losing the ability to speak. Being diagnosed with a neuro-degenerative disease like ALS. The death of a child or the murder of a loved one. When these things happen, we have no choice but to make a change.

Keep in mind this relative context as you go through the book; it may help you anticipate or understand some of the things that occur around a particular crisis. But recognize that *your own* experience, assumptions, and resources influence where *you* would place a particular crisis on the chart.

Who is involved in the crisis?

In this book, we're going to look primarily at three groups of people (see Figure 2):

The individual in crisis – This is the person in the bull's-eye, the person who has experienced the main shock from the crisis—the person who lost the job, or had the heart attack, or got divorced.

Members of the "inner circle" – When we talk about the inner circle, we usually mean immediate family members and close friends. Often they are the ones who act as caregivers (for example, taking care of a sick spouse) and can feel as though they are in crisis as well. In fact, depending on the circumstance, sometimes they may feel more distress than the person in crisis.

Members of the "outer circle" – These people are typically extended family members, friends, and the broader community, such as neighbors and colleagues, surrounding the individual in crisis.

The closer you are to the center of the crisis, the harder it is to maintain stability and perspective. The further away you are, the easier it is. With that small insight, the importance of both the inner circle and outer circle becomes more evident.

Figure 2 Roles and Proximity to Crisis

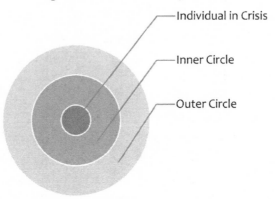

Individual in Crisis

Inner Circle

Outer Circle

What happens to a person in crisis?

Shock has the tendency to bring out extremes. Physically, some of us can't sleep and are constantly exhausted; others are wired and jumpy. Some of us can't stop eating; others can't take a bite or even forget to eat. Mentally, we may experience hyperclarity in the actual moment of crisis, but in the aftermath we frequently have difficulty with focus, concentration, and decision making. Emotionally, we often become hypersensitive, easily swinging between tears and anger. Sometimes we have an extreme need to surround ourselves with other people; other times we isolate ourselves.

While each person reacts in his or her own way to a crisis, there are some common patterns you may see. Take a look at Figure 3, which lists common reactions. Which have you experienced or observed?

Figure 3 Common Characteristics of a Person in Crisis

Physical
- Change in sleeping patterns; extremes of more or less
- Fatigue or hyperactivity
- Change in eating patterns; extremes of more or less
- Acute pain or chronic discomfort (digestive, muscular, neurological, etc.)
- Decreased immunity resulting in infections ranging from minor to severe
- Increased sensitivity to physical surroundings (temperature, noise level, humidity, proximity to co-workers, etc.)

Mental
- Difficulty with concentration or focus on the task at hand
- Decreased listening skills and/or ability to focus on the speaker
- Difficulty with absorbing and/or retaining information
- Difficulty with logic and continuation through a process
- Difficulty with decision making, poor decision making, or inability to make decisions
- Periodic but unsustainable hyperclarity

Emotional
- Heightened emotional responses, including but not limited to tearfulness, anger, irritability
- Heightened ego sensitivity, including but not limited to feeling attacked and misunderstood or feeling the need to defend oneself
- Exaggerated communication patterns ranging from silence to talking non-stop
- General sense of feeling overwhelmed
- Extremes of either accepting all blame or no blame for problems or mistakes
- Varying and sometimes unpredictable needs for solitude or community
- Uncertainty about role or worth in the future

Spiritual
- Either questioning religious beliefs or staunchly defending them
- Either searching for answers to "why" or denying a need for them
- Stronger alignment with or disengagement from religious groups

How do people respond to different types of crisis?

In the prior section we looked at characteristics we may see exhibited by someone in the midst of crisis. In Figure 4, you'll find some common responses to the four types of crisis from the person in the bull's-eye, the inner circle, and the outer circle.

You'll see some commonality between difficult situations and acute crises, regardless of whose response it is. This is primarily related to length of time. We all tend to handle short-term stresses better than long-term stresses. We can maintain the mindset "This too shall pass" for a while.

You may also note that individuals in crisis and members of the inner circle have common responses in chronic and life-altering crises. By contrast, the outer circle can fade away over time during chronic crises, and may disappear completely if a life-altering change is too uncomfortable to be around.

I'll repeat myself: this is only a model. While these general patterns appear frequently, responses from any box may show up in your crisis situation. But it's useful to have a base for understanding what *may* happen so you can 1) prepare for it, 2) recognize it if it does happen, and 3) choose how you want to respond.

QUESTION FOR REFLECTION

What reactions have I observed in myself or others in crisis?

Figure 4 Common Responses to Different Types of Crisis by Role

	Individual in Crisis	Inner Circle	Outer Circle
Difficulty (Small fire)	• Feel surge of anxiety or clarity • Feel comfort and control affected • Feel the problem can be handled eventually	• Pull together • Do whatever it takes • Understand resources needed	• Offer help within limits • Require clear direction • Assess connection to the individual or situation to decide level of involvement
Acute Crisis (Temporary job loss)	• Experience panic, confusion, or bewilderment • Feel fear of death or permanent loss • Find unanticipated calm	• Either pull together or watch a solitary hero emerge • Do whatever it takes • Desire to be either hands-on doer or hands-off adviser	• Offer help within limits • Require clear direction • Assess connection to the individual or situation to decide level of involvement
Chronic Crisis (HIV diagnosis)	• Cope well, or complain • Become either a victim or a crusader regarding the problem • Pursue outward focus to avoid self-focus as well as to retain connection to others	• Feel sustainability of relationships and resources tested • Develop effective coping systems • Become silent or vocal martyr • Feel desire for interests outside the chronic problem • Experience shift in roles	• When called on, initially offer help willingly • Have occasional short-term involvement, but often get tired and fade away over time • Feel guilt or shame for not doing more • Don't realize an issue still exists
Life-Altering Change (Limb amputation)	• Experience post-traumatic stress or post-traumatic growth • Experience either depression or a heightened reason for being • Enter new communities • Increase search for meaning and connection beyond self	• Find relationships either torn apart or cemented • Develop effective coping strategies • Change priorities • Become involved with new communities • Experience shift in roles	• Become comfortable with changes and have normal relationship with individual in crisis • Feel too uncomfortable for direct involvement • Champion a cause on behalf of the individual • Discontinue all connection

WHAT DO WE MEAN BY *RESILIENCE?*

Merriam-Webster offers multiple definitions of *resilience.* The one that speaks best to this text is "The ability to become strong, healthy, or successful again after something bad happens."

In *The Human Dimensions of Resilience,* Terri I. Sivilli and Thaddeus W. W. Pace offer a broader perspective. "Resilience isn't just one thing; it's a cluster of qualities and traits that allows us to respond effectively to life's challenges."

> *Resilience isn't just one thing; it's a cluster of qualities and traits that allows us to respond effectively to life's challenges.*

Have you heard *resilience* described as "the ability to bounce back"? Have you seen it illustrated as the bouncy doll weighted heavily on the bottom so that when it is knocked down, it bounces right back up? While that description highlights the "undefeated" aspect of resilience, in my experience, resilient people rely on a combination of strengths, and thus demonstrate a more sustainable quality: *they move on through.*

Resilient people move on through pain. Resilient people move on through financial hardship. Resilient people move on through broken relationships, job loss, and grief. They move on through unanswered questions or crises piling up on top of each other. In the midst of moving on, resilient people may stumble, fall back, or get stuck, but eventually they move on.

In our goal-oriented society, we focus on positive end points—landing a great job, finding our true love, raising wonderful children, or even winning the lottery. Those are all good things, but life is about more than end points. An ancient Hebrew proverb states, "The journey is our home." At its best, "home" means safety and security, the place where we return when it gets dark outside. If our life's journey is where we really live, then we must discover how we can move through all the "rooms" in the house of life, especially those that contain fear or confusion.

What's the difference between Reaction and Resilience?

We talked above about how crisis brings out extremes in behavior. One manifestation of that is our tendency to *react*. (Consider the related term "reactionary," which describes an extreme political position.) Now of course when a stimulus is applied, we are going to react. You poke me with a needle and I holler. But in this case we're talking about not just automatic reactions, but those automatic reactions that tend to be defensive and often negative in nature. The fight-or-flight response takes over.

By comparison, if we can take a moment to *think* when hit with something unexpected, we are more likely to *respond* rather than to react. Responding is a more resilient approach than reacting is. But remember how hard it is to think in crisis?

Let's face it, most of us will simply react when a crisis hits. That's OK. It's human nature. Once we react, we can start moving on toward resilience. The *After the Shock* process gives you multiple ways to strengthen your resilience while you are moving through and beyond crisis. Figure 5 offers some examples of what a *reaction* might look like compared to what a more *resilient response* might look like in a variety of crisis situations.

QUESTION FOR REFLECTION

What resilient responses have I observed in myself or others in crisis?

Figure 5 Reaction vs. Resilience in Crisis

Situation	Reaction	Resilient Response
Difficulty Being over-looked for promotion	• Verbal confrontation with boss • Complaining to co-workers • Resigning in anger	• Debriefing intense emotions privately • Gathering information on why overlooked and how to adjust • Enlisting a mentor
Acute Crisis Divorce	• Confrontations with ex • Trying to get people to take sides • Entering immediately into a new relationship ("rebounding")	• Processing intense feelings with neutral party • Maintaining distance • Keeping neutral attitude in public towards ex
Chronic Crisis Diabetes	• Pretending diagnosis is wrong • Ignoring doctor's advice • Obsessing about blood sugar or other stats	• Learning and practicing healthy eating and exercise habits • Joining a support group for information and encouragement
Life-Altering Change Alzheimer's diagnosis	• Despair, feeling that life is already over or mind is already gone • Denial of diagnosis and maintaining activities that are no longer safe (e.g., driving)	• Making plans and choices about future care • Doing the meaningful and enjoyable things that are still possible

AFTER THE SHOCK™ MODEL OVERVIEW

Let's look at a brief overview of the model we'll be using throughout the book as well as an analogy to tie it all together. The model has two main components: The Four Cs of Stability and the E-A-R Road to Resilience.

The Four Cs of Stability

Part 1 of this book focuses on four fundamental human concerns that we'll call the Four Cs of Stability:

- ❖ **Comfort** – I want to be free from pain and constraint, physically and emotionally.
- ❖ **Control** – I want the power to make my own decisions and manage how things are done.
- ❖ **Community** – I want to share my life with other people.
- ❖ **Connection** – I want to feel a bond with something bigger than myself.

These Four Cs are our foundation. They give us balance, strength, and support. They create stability. They are core needs that come into play throughout our lives, but particularly when we're in crisis. We usually have to stabilize before we can proceed toward resilience.

The E-A-R Road to Resilience

Once we've stabilized using the Four Cs, we can start moving more actively towards resilience. Part 2 of this book offers a process that helps us move toward a more resilient response:

- ❖ **Experience** – How do I understand and use my own experience or that of others to deal with this crisis?
- ❖ **Assumptions** – How do I hold healthy assumptions that will support me through this crisis?
- ❖ **Resources** – What resources do I already have to help me move through this crisis? What resources do I need? What resources do I need to learn to live without?

I Can't Resist a Good Metaphor: The Vehicle of Life

I like using pictures in my work. Pictures take our words and not only add clarity but open up new spaces in our minds. In thinking about the approach used in *After the Shock*, I realized that crisis is indeed where the rubber hits the road in our lives. So what better illustration could there be than the vehicle that takes us down the road? A car.

Take a look at the Four Cs of Stability. What image comes to your mind? I see tires. Like tires, these four Cs balance each other in sets of two. The front tires are Comfort and Control. Most of us want to be comfortable—free from pain and constraint. We may not say we want control, but deep inside we realize we're more stable when we control at least a part of life. The rear tires get us out of the mud and give us some traction: Community and Connection to something beyond ourselves. We may not think about them a lot, but they give us more *oomph* than we have on our own.

If you picture the Four Cs as four tires, you've got the base that takes you down the road of life. The road may be smooth, bumpy, or marred by potholes, but the stability of those tires (along with some shock absorbers) will help even out the ride. Poor driving experiences and road conditions may throw our tires out of alignment, cause a flat, or make a wheel fall off completely, but those problems can be corrected. The same thing is true about our Four Cs. When life is calm and easy, our Four Cs self-adjust; when things get rocky, we need to pay attention to keep them inflated and aligned.

Tires are great, but by themselves they don't get us anywhere. A car's got to have a frame. When we think about shock, Experience is what frames our thoughts and actions. I find there are several helpful questions about Experience:

❖ Have I been through this or something parallel to it before?

❖ If so, what have I learned that is useful or that could help me right now?

❖ If this experience is totally new to me, who do I know or what do I trust that will give me the information I need to move forward safely?

To guide your car down the road, you need a steering wheel and the drive shaft that goes with it. I compare that to the Assumptions that guide or influence us. Assumptions can be positive or not so positive; they can head us in a direction we want to go, or they can steer us away from our intended destination. Again, we have questions that help us examine our assumptions and decide whether they are useful in this crisis:

❖ Is this assumption authentic for me right now?

❖ Is this assumption empowering and supportive for me right now?

❖ Is this assumption heading me in the direction I want to go?

If a prevailing assumption doesn't meet those criteria, then we can decide if we want to do a little repair work on it, pack it up and put it in the trunk temporarily, or pitch it out permanently.

We've got a great car put together, but it won't get very far without fuel. Our Resources—physical, financial, social, or internal—fuel this vehicle. *After the Shock* helps you look at the resources you have, the resources you need, and what you may have to learn to live without. We may also have to look at whether we must change fuels. My old car ran on diesel, but now I've got a hybrid, so diesel will no longer cut it. The same is true with crisis: each experience requires different resources.

One thing I've observed repeatedly: individuals and organizations want to bypass all the other parts of the car and jump immediately to fuel (Resources) to correct or address a crisis. That makes as much sense as standing at the gas station with two tires by the garage, two tires at the edge of the road, the frame of the car at the next pump, and the steering wheel at your feet, while spraying gas all over the separate parts. And you wonder why the car won't go down the road!

To move forward smoothly during and after a shock, start from the ground up, put the parts together, and *then* provide the fuel. Remember, the goal is not to be immediately OK, but rather to stabilize, then to move *toward* OK—or even toward "better." With all the parts of your Vehicle of Life assembled and fueled up, you can begin your journey from reaction to resilience.

> *The goal is not to be immediately OK, but rather to stabilize, then to move toward OK—or even toward "better."*

Part 1:
The Four Cs of Stability

Comfort: Freedom from Pain and Constraint
Control: Power to Manage Your Life
Community: Sharing Your Life
Connection: Finding Greater Meaning

Comfort:
Freedom from Pain and Constraint

*Life is made up, not of great sacrifices or duties, but of little things,
in which smiles and kindness, and small obligations given
habitually, are what preserve the heart and secure comfort.*
—Humphry Davy, British scientist and poet, 1778-1829

Recently I had coffee with my friend Gwen, whose husband, Richard, has been chronically ill for years. She told me Richard was having trouble sleeping at night. I went through my mental checklist and asked Gwen some simple questions. Was he dealing with nightmares? Hallucinations? Sleepwalking? No. No. No.

"He calls out," Gwen said, "but he isn't saying anything. He's just restless."

The word "restless" caught my ear. I encouraged her to talk some more. She repeated what she had already told me.

Then I asked, "Do you think he might be in pain?"

Gwen snapped back, "No. I've told you over and over, he's not in pain. That's been one of the few good things about this awful disease. Even though he's been sick for so long, I'm thankful he doesn't need pain medicine." For years Richard had defied doctors' predictions of his more immediate decline.

But something else crossed my mind. If Richard *is* in pain, things may be changing. And that change may be uncomfortable—and probably scary—for Richard *and* Gwen.

I gently said, "Well, I'm not a nurse, but I have heard the nurses say that *sometimes* people get restless like you're describing when they're in pain, but they don't know how to say it. Or they're too sleepy to say it. Or they're just not used to talking about pain. *Sometimes* if they take the medicine the doctor suggests, they can get some rest. Then the next day is better," I paused, "for both of you."

Gwen's face relaxed. Suddenly the situation shifted from "If he has pain, he might be dying" to "This will help him rest better at night."

WHAT DO WE MEAN BY *COMFORT*?

Merriam-Webster defines *comfort* as:

1. A state or situation in which you are relaxed and do not have any physically unpleasant feelings caused by pain, heat, cold, etc., or

2. A state or feeling of being less worried, upset, frightened, etc., during a time of trouble or emotional pain.

Gwen and Richard's story touches on two aspects of comfort: the physical and the emotional.

Richard certainly appeared to have some sort of physical discomfort that needed to be addressed. Gwen (and likely Richard too) had intense emotional discomfort. The situation they'd been in for many years—managing a chronic illness—had suddenly shifted to something more acute. In spite of everything they had been through, this was a new shock to their system. The trick was to find a way to address both the physical and the emotional discomfort: medication for Richard and a reframing of the situation for Gwen.

Possible Indicators of Comfort/Discomfort	
Comfort	**Discomfort**
♦ A relaxed or smiling face	♦ Frown or furrowed brow; grimace
♦ Slower, deeper breathing	♦ Shallow or tight breathing
♦ Relaxed yawn	♦ Restlessness
♦ Laughter	♦ Silence or caustic communication
♦ Relaxed or casual posture	♦ Tense muscles; clenched fists

The Value of Comfort

Why is comfort important? Picture this: You find yourself in a mysterious location where people speak a language you don't understand. They shove you from one place to another, finally leaving you alone in a room that feels like a freezer—and you don't have a jacket. Sounds pretty miserable, doesn't it? But isn't that what some people experience in a hospital emergency room?

We take basic elements of comfort for granted. We assume that every day will include simple communication, normal

Simple comforts that merely satisfy us in normal times may sustain us in times of crisis.

socialization, and whatever we need to make life reasonably pleasant. We don't focus on comfort because we don't need to. We're comfortable enough to function just fine.

When a crisis throws us into a miserable spot, not only does some part of us feel bad, but we also "freeze up" physically, mentally, emotionally, or spiritually.

Go back to the emergency room. Notice the difference if a doctor uses words you understand, aides gently move you from a gurney to an X-ray table, and a nurse wraps an extra blanket around your shivering body. Can you feel yourself beginning to relax a little bit?

Whether something soothes the skin, the stomach, or the heart, it separates us briefly from the clutch of the crisis, allowing us to rest and refocus.

Talking Around Comfort

Talking about comfort can feel odd. Sometimes when we talk about money, we hear people say "I don't want to be rich, I just want to be comfortable." What does that mean? Financial planners wrestle with this question with their clients. Generally, most people want a sense their physical and emotional needs are met. Regardless of how we describe it, the need for comfort is inherent within us.

When we encounter shock, whether momentary or on-going, many things get very uncomfortable. The problem is, we're not good at talking about them. Richard had trouble discussing his physical discomfort. Maybe he didn't recognize his discomfort while he was trying to sleep, so was less able to talk about it, but many of us talk *around* the issue of comfort.

People rarely say, "I want to be comfortable" (financial example above notwithstanding). When people are in pain, they are more likely to say, "I don't want to hurt." But when asked by a nurse if they are hurting, they often say, "No." Yet they may show other symptoms, such as fidgetiness or trouble sleeping that *they* don't identify as pain—but their body *does*.

This hesitance to voice our desire for comfort is partly cultural. In the United States we are largely a "stiff upper lip" group. The standard answer to "How are you?" is "Fine" or "OK," especially if the person asking is not in our inner circle.

When people *do* talk about being comfortable, they often are referring to *things that bring them comfort*. It may be a nightgown that is soft on the skin or a blanket to cuddle under or emotional comfort from the people around them. It may be an old pair of slippers.

We don't talk about these forms of self-care because, in general, our society reinforces the notion that people who intentionally pursue comfort are narcissistic and selfish. We forget about the *healthy* understanding of this word.

> *Begin now to identify what comforts you—it's not only OK, it's important.*

We use the phrase "comfort food," and we recognize the importance of food in comforting the anxious or grieving person. I noticed frequently in my hospice work that food brought comfort *even when someone couldn't eat.* Patients with limited appetites still talked about memories, traditions, and family gatherings focused on particular foods. They reminisced about familiar foods and the celebrations in which food was almost an honored guest. Patients described dishes they or their mother or their grandmother made. Even when the food could no longer be eaten, it still retained its status as comfort food.

Begin *now* to identify what comforts you in different parts of your life. Not only is it OK to identify these elements, it's important. Return to the metaphor of four tires as stabilizers for your car, then picture Comfort as one of the stabilizers for your life. Just as you need to know what tires work best on your car, you need to know what comfort measures work best for you.

Things That May Bring Comfort

People or Animals
- Spouse
- Children
- Grandchildren
- Best friend
- Colleagues
- Pet(s)

Physical Things
- A piece of clothing (warm PJs, old sweatshirt)
- Favorite food(s)
- Pictures
- Religious symbols
- Special locations (beach, lake, mountains)

Actions or Activities
- Cuddling under a blanket
- A hot bath
- A shoulder rub
- Watching or playing a sport
- Listening to music
- Playing a card game
- Watching a favorite TV show or movie
- Gardening

QUESTIONS FOR REFLECTION

When I am in pain or upset, what helps me relax and feel at ease? What comforts me when things are rough?

Being w/ all of us together

Do I need anything on that list right now?

If so, can I take care of it myself, or would it be better to ask for some help?

Comfort Is Personal

While food may be a universal example of a way to experience comfort, each individual has her own preferences. Here in the South, banana pudding is considered comfort food. If you put a bowl of banana pudding in front of me, I would gag. Why? Preferences are based on our individual experiences. I was raised in Yankee territory, so I didn't grow up with banana pudding being associated with comfort. For me, comfort equals Mom's meatloaf smothered with ketchup.

The need for comfort is less dependent on the situation and more on the person *in* the situation. One person may struggle with overwhelm in circumstances that cause only irritation for another.

When I began this book, a friend was helping me talk through the content. We wanted to record our phone conversations and chose an online service that required us to install an application on our computers.

Now let me just say, I am not a tech savvy person. I didn't grow up with it; I had to learn everything as an adult; I frequently call the Geek Squad® for help. Technology. Makes. Me. Nervous.

I tried and tried and tried to get the application installed and working. No luck. Frustration galore.

I grabbed the phone, called my friend, and poured out my woes.

Calmly she said, "No problem. Let me install it." After a brief pause she continued, "Oh, I see what you mean. I'm getting the same problem. Let me just play with this a minute... OK, this should work for now. I'll see if I can figure out how to fix yours later."

The same problem that caused me anxiety and embarrassment due to my sense of incompetence was for her simply a blip in the normal workday. Little did I know she used to provide tech support, define software requirements, and test software. She had a completely different experience with technology than I did—and an assumption that she could solve technical problems with a little experimentation.

Physical Pain vs. Emotional Pain

Usually raw, often misunderstood, and intensely intimate, emotional pain highlights our vulnerability as much as or more than physical pain. Piercing through our perceived ability to handle life, and racing down to our shame of inadequacy, emotional pain can break our heart, twist our gut, and leave us without the imaginary badge of honor that gets bestowed on physical pain. To complicate matters even more, our culture teaches little boys not to cry and little girls to pick their crying locations carefully.

When it comes to physical pain, the medical community has created a simple assessment tool that helps patients express the degree of discomfort they are feeling. Doctors and nurses ask patients to rate their pain on a scale of one to ten, giving examples of what the numbers represent. This linear model works well when translating an intangible experience like pain into a measurable item.

However, for emotional pain, based on the complexity of possible responses, I think we should use a multiple-choice circle rather than a select-one-answer linear assessment. In the Crisis Wheel of Emotion (Figure 6) I placed the words we normally consider "positive" on the right and "negative" on the left. The emotions that affect the way we function are on the bottom, while those that reflect our state of well-being are on the top.

Shock-related emotions sometimes appear the way we expect them to, but sometimes they don't. *A person may experience a mixture of emotions from several parts of the wheel simultaneously.* Emotional pain may respond well to simple comfort measures, may need skilled therapeutic intervention, may return with different symptoms, or may gradually subside as other conditions improve.

Figure 6 Crisis Wheel of Emotion

Well-being

⌐ Disbelief Bitterness Self-pity Regret Heartbreak	Acceptance Contentment Gratitude Satisfaction Joy
Panic Confusion Apprehension Irritation Isolation	Calm Clarity Confidence Serenity Connection

Function

Reshard talked to me months after his house burned to the ground from a lightning strike. He expressed gratitude that he and his family were on vacation at the time, with their beloved dog safely boarded at the kennel. As we talked, I saw Reshard's body become increasingly tense. His hands drew up into fists, while his voice stayed calm and his words remained "I'm so grateful" and "It could have been worse."

When I asked Reshard what he was feeling, he burst out, "I feel like I'm about to explode. At night I wake up in a cold sweat thinking about what could have happened. Then I say a prayer of thanks that we're OK. Then I get mad at our insurance company for fighting us on part of the payout, but I feel guilty because I haven't really read the policy in years. I try to go back to sleep, but these feelings keep crashing into each other."

The Crisis Wheel of Emotion is not a simplistic way to show a logical flow of correct emotional patterns, but rather a simple representation of the wide variety of responses shock elicits. The wheel is intended to create awareness of both the differences and the proximity of these profound feelings. Some of them require a lot of Comfort.

QUESTIONS FOR REFLECTION

Does anything on the Crisis Wheel of Emotion fit what you are feeling? all the negatives in varying degrees gratitude - no more suffering the inescaple pains life brings - but then no more joy either & he felt so much joy. Happened at home not driving

If not, can you describe what you are feeling? (This can be multiple feelings, and they don't need to fit a pattern.) fearful often, alone in my world of "being" thoughts & emotions.. Standing still, existing, fearful of next moments, pain from my fall, fatigue in general lack of motivation & then motivated - vascillates

What/who could bring comfort to the feelings that are hurting or upsetting you right now? family, Elise, close friends in small doses. Massage, hot baths,

Reward yourself after you have taken action on the last question. You are re-inflating the tire of Comfort on your Vehicle of Life.

FINDING COMFORT FOR YOURSELF

When I work with people in crisis, one of the first things I do is help them create a sense of normalcy, which enhances both Comfort and Control (more about Control in the next chapter). A simple way to create normalcy is to bring everyday objects and activities back into your life. Some of the most powerful Comfort remedies involve rituals and traditions.

Rituals

Habits are repetitive actions we take, often without thinking and sometimes almost involuntarily (Merriam-Webster). Have you ever arrived at work and not been able to remember the drive? That's due to habit.

Rituals are also repetitive, but they are *conscious* actions. They follow a social custom or particular protocol; they are done in a particular situation and in the same way each time (Merriam-Webster). Whether ritual involves the way we get dressed in the morning, the things we do in our family life, or the activities that come from religious or cultural practices, they bring comfort. When things feel really crazy for my clients (or for me), one of the first things I do is ask, "Is there a ritual that will comfort you right now?"

Ritual is one reason smokers have so much trouble quitting. Besides the actual physical addiction, smoking is often associated with a meal, reading the newspaper, or having coffee with friends. Just as bringing a ritual back into everyday life brings comfort, removing a ritual causes discomfort.

I knew a couple who took a two-week vacation every summer by themselves (no children and no pets!). Part of Heath and Georgia's ritual included laying out intricate plans for the trip. All through the winter they pulled out travel information and maps and books (in the days before Google). The other part of the annual ritual, of course, was the trip itself and all the things they enjoyed along the way—food, wine, sightseeing.

But the loss of Heath's job upended their normal plans, so I suggested that they plan a virtual trip. I encouraged them to do those things they would have done through the winter — getting beautiful literature and talking about all the things they wanted to see — and doing it all very intentionally. They followed my advice, planned their trip to Florence, Italy, and became world travelers while staying at home. They downloaded a video about Florence that took them on a walking tour from the San Lorenzo Market to the Medici Chapel to the Piazzale Michelangelo. Not to miss out on the exquisite food, Georgia researched recipes and created several meals they would have savored in Tuscany. Since they were staying at home, they could even splurge on a great bottle of wine!

Heath and Georgia maintained their annual ritual, albeit in an adapted form. And since it was such a complex ritual, it kept them positively engaged for a long time. This reconstructed ritual provided beautiful images, tasty cuisine, and the comforting stability of honoring an annual commitment to their special time as a couple.

Fortunately, rituals don't have to be nearly that complex to soothe and stabilize us. Any special part of normal life that can be reinstated directly or indirectly can be hugely helpful in providing comfort.

Traditions

Likewise, maintaining traditions can be beneficial. Traditions are "a way of thinking, behaving, or doing something that has been used by the people in a particular group, family, society, etc., for a long time" or "the stories, beliefs, etc., that have been part of the culture of a group of people for a long time" (Merriam-Webster). They may include a particular type of holiday celebration (e.g., wearing traditional African clothing for Kwanzaa), participation at sporting events (e.g., tailgating with friends or alumni), or following a family career path (e.g., serving in the military).

In one of the families I served as a hospice chaplain, the grandmother came from Sweden, where it was traditional to bake all kind of treats *A surprising amount of comfort can come from very little things.* around the winter holidays. Unfortunately her illness prevented her from baking during what was to be her final holiday season.

Instead, her hospice team was able to help her enlist her grandchildren as her cooking arm. In this way she benefited twofold: 1) she kept her tradition of creating special holiday cookies, and 2) she was able to pass on that tradition directly to her grandchildren. Everyone received comfort on a variety of levels: the delightful smell of cookies hot out of the oven, the continuity of life as they were used to it, and the special comfort of passing on a tradition to the next generation. I happened to be there the day after the big baking adventure. I got to share their joy…and their cookies!

Whether you reinstitute an old tradition, reconstitute one to fit the new situation, or create a new tradition, a surprising amount of comfort can come from what are sometimes very little things.

QUESTIONS FOR REFLECTION

What rituals or traditions are important to me? Thanksgiving w/. the Rao's, walking in nature,

What rituals or traditions could I consider starting or restarting to bring comfort?

Finding a Catalyst for Comfort

When I think of pain and comfort, I often think of Luis. Luis was a man's man. He'd worked in the construction industry. He'd used his hands. He'd always been a stoic, stalwart, do-it-yourself kind of guy. Luis considered himself moderately religious. He attended church, and it was part of his family's life, but he seldom discussed matters of faith.

Luis had bone cancer, which can be very painful even with the best of medical care. He eventually took medication, which helped relieve some of the pain, but not all of it.

Think back to your high school chemistry lab, when you had two chemicals that could work together to create something new but needed a catalyst to start the reaction. Luis found that having a catalyst allowed his medication to bring him more comfort.

When Luis was having a challenging time, his wife Renata would ask me to read to him from the Bible. Now Renata, by her own admission, had a high-pitched, "tinny" voice. She said there was something about my voice that was much more comfortable to Luis's ear. "When you read the Bible to Luis," she said, "it helps him relax and get comfortable enough that the medicine can start to work."

Sometimes we need a variety of things working together to bring comfort. Whether it's music, white noise, or something we touch, a catalyst can take our mind off things so positive factors can come into play. Luis's catalyst was my voice.

HELPING SOMEONE ELSE FIND COMFORT

As we go through a crisis, keeping potential sources of comfort in mind for ourselves is beneficial. But sometimes we are not the one "walking the path." To help others find comfort, we first may need to help them acknowledge and name their pain.

Naming the Pain

Craig Abernathy lived straight and talked straight. When he realized his chemotherapy treatments made him miserable but were not going to cure him, he said, "That's enough." He chose hospice care, and I became his chaplain.

Craig told many stories about his family, but he rarely mentioned his brother, Dennis, from whom he was estranged.

One day I finally said, "I wonder if it hurts that you and your brother haven't talked for thirty years." Making this kind of speculative comment made me nervous. Sometimes in response a patient would be direct ("Yes, it is really bad") or would begin to describe the circumstances around the pain ("I tried calling, and he never called back"). But sometimes he would avoid the topic at all costs, even to the point of anger.

In Craig's case, he began to explain the circumstances. Something had been said at their mother's funeral. Emotions were running high and the entire family was at its most sensitive spot. As is typical in situations like this, Craig couldn't even remember the initial issue with his brother.

Then I asked another potentially dangerous question: "Would it help to talk to him?"

No! He wasn't going down that path. He wasn't going to acknowledge the pain at all.

I continued to press gently, "Sometimes at this point in life, people like to mend their fences. It can be a healthy, good thing to do."

That got us to a secondary layer: protection against the pain.

"I don't think he'd want to talk to me," Craig said.

"That may be true," I responded, "but sometimes it's just awkward, and someone has to take the first step. You strike me as a pretty direct person. You're used to saying what's on your mind and just taking care of things. You might have to be the one to take that first step."

Eventually Craig agreed that it would be all right for his wife to make a call to his brother's house and say that Craig would like to talk to Dennis, if Dennis would be open to it. *If he will, I will.*

After thirty-two years, Craig and Dennis finally spoke. All the pain and wounds did not go away, but in their conversation they found an element of healing.

Sometimes people will allow the healing to happen, and sometimes they won't. Sometimes they will take medications, and sometimes they won't. Sometimes a person will sprain her ankle and go get it properly taped, but sometimes she hobbles along saying, "I'm OK."

Even the person who is hobbling probably would like help, but she has two pains at odds—the physical pain of the sprained ankle and the pain of admitting she needs help. If she can tolerate the ankle pain better than she can tolerate a bruised ego, she may elect to continue hobbling. If Craig could tolerate the pain of separation from Dennis more than he could tolerate the pain of being the first to extend a hand, the brothers may never have reconciled.

Want to decrease your pain? First admit you have some.

We humans may sometimes use internal logic that does not make sense to others, but, to paraphrase our Twelve-Step friends, the first step in addressing pain is to acknowledge it exists.

Careful Listening

To help someone who is in crisis or dealing with any type of pain, careful listening is one of the best tools. Most of us aren't used to listening closely. We're doing a variety of things at once, and our minds race ahead in the conversation. If you slow down and listen attentively, the person speaking will often use a word that gives insight about where she is or what she is feeling. As you gain some experience, key words will hit your ear. And you don't have to be a trained counselor or chaplain for that to happen.

Asking Questions

As simple as it sounds, careful listening starts with asking questions in a way that takes the discussion deeper.

Say you have a friend who is ill. She says she's OK, but a little jittery. You might say, "Help me understand what this is like for you. What does it feel like when you are jittery? What happens?" She might say she is shaky, or nervous, or can't find good place to sit/lie/stretch. You might say, "Can you tell me more about that?"

So you might find out that "jittery" is tied to something physical—your friend can't sit or lie comfortably. But "jittery" might also be related to the times her sister-in-law comes to visit. Or when the next-door neighbor comes to stay while her husband is out on an errand; the neighbor might have some habit that makes your friend uncomfortable.

There are so many possibilities for "jittery" that you have to be a detective. I call it "playing Columbo." On the way to the door after questioning his suspect, the rumpled detective would turn around and say, "Just one more thing..."and ask his question. Particularly with pain, you have to sleuth it out, because we're not taught to talk about pain. We are brave boys and girls.

Permission to Speak

Often, it is most effective to ask questions and let the person speaking come to his own conclusions and realizations. But sometimes you may get to the point where you need to state something or explain what you see going on.

In our example with Craig above, I made the statement "I wonder if it hurts that you and your brother haven't talked for thirty years." Though carefully couched, this statement went beyond an inquiry or reflection. It introduced an original idea, an idea not initiated by Craig. I could make this statement because I had built up trust with Craig and I had *permission* to speak.

No one likes to be told how they feel or what they "should" do. When making statements of this sort, in addition to having permission, it is useful to use phrases that soften the statement, such as "It dawns on me that..." or "It sounds like..." Offer your idea as a supposition or a possibility. You'll find out quickly if you're on target, off target, or on target but the person doesn't want to acknowledge it. Your thought might initiate a new awareness for the individual — "Oh, I hadn't thought about it like that."

Or, you may find the real issue differs from the presenting problem. Richard, at the beginning of this chapter, exhibited restlessness; his real issue was pain.

Working with Family

Working directly with someone in crisis is complicated enough. It can get even more complicated when dealing with that person's family members. They are dealing with a loved one in pain (physical and/or emotional), and they bring their own sets of experiences and assumptions. They need the same sort of careful listening and comfort you might offer the person in crisis. And sometimes you may need to help them dissect whether their actions are in sync with the wishes of the person in crisis. Whether medical treatment, financial decisions, legal advice, or other areas of decision making, the focus should be on *that* person's preferences to the extent possible.

> Being a family member doesn't mean you can read the mind of the person in crisis. Ask questions.

Marilyn's divorce turned ugly when her ex-husband, Chuck, lost money in a bad business investment. Chuck petitioned the court to reduce child support by twenty percent. Marilyn panicked, called her brother, Toby, and wailed, "I don't know how I'll make it!" Always protective, Toby growled, "He'll pay."

By the next day, Marilyn realized she had overreacted. Her ex-husband had originally offered child support well above the legal requirement. Whether his generosity sprang from guilt or goodness, Marilyn didn't care; she had accepted the agreement on behalf of their two children. With this pending adjustment, she would receive the legally required amount, but no more. While a few luxuries would have to go, Marilyn *could* meet her budget on the reduced amount and continue to work only part-time, allowing her to fulfill her greatest joy— being an attentive mother to her ten- and twelve-year-old daughters.

The bigger problem was Toby. He wanted revenge against the man who hurt "sweet Marilyn." Despite Marilyn's pleas that she wanted a peaceful divorce more than she wanted a few extra dollars, Toby felt compelled to intervene on behalf of his kid sister.

Marilyn begged a trusted mutual friend to mediate this painful family squabble. Eventually, Toby heard from their friend what he couldn't hear from his sister. Marilyn wanted resolution more than revenge and conclusion more than cash. Toby retreated when he understood that having enough money to pay her bills, time to spend with her daughters, and avoiding a legal battle equaled comfort for Marilyn.

Working with Professional Personnel

Not only do families' attitudes come into play, but so do the opinions of professional personnel.

With an ill patient, physicians and nurses want to provide the best clinical care, while respecting the patient's wishes. Ultimately, however, medical personnel are still people whose beliefs, traditions, and mores come into play. For example, they sometimes fear speeding up a very ill patient's death and, as a result, may underdose morphine or other painkillers.

In a divorce case, the attorneys for the divorcing parties play a huge role in how smoothly the dissolution proceeds. An attorney whose position is "Let's find a fair settlement" will take different actions from one whose attitude is "Go for the jugular." Alignment with client attitudes is critical.

Adult children often find themselves helping their parents with financial matters. Again, this is a vital area in which professionals and family members must understand and honor the primary client's financial priorities. That may include spending money to take the family on a dream vacation, even when the children think it would be better to save the funds for potential healthcare or nursing home expenses.

The important thing in all of these types of crises (and in non-crisis situations as well) is to help the family and professional personnel recognize and understand what the person in crisis wants.

Returning to Marilyn's story, the trusted family friend who resolved the quarrel between Marilyn and her brother had also previously helped Marilyn find an attorney. Known for his firm but collaborative style, the lawyer represented Marilyn's principles as well as her legal rights. This allowed her to conclude a difficult chapter of her life more comfortably and move ahead with greater ease.

HIGHLIGHT STORY:
DON'T MOVE OR YOU COULD DIE

Happily married to Steve, finishing her master's degree in social work, and settled into an old Victorian home outside Boston, Laurie Ray had a comfortable life. One Saturday while her airline-pilot husband was flying from New York to Boston, Laurie relaxed in a leisurely bath before a planned brunch with friends. Suddenly she felt a stabbing headache.

She got out of the tub to take some Tylenol, but when she returned to the warm water, the pain worsened. She realized it was more than just a headache. As she leaned against the tub, her left side collapsed. She managed to call her friend Cate, who lived nearby. While waiting for Cate, she struggled out of the tub. Unable to dry off, she tried to put on a robe, then slid to the floor. She couldn't crawl to the phone to dial 9-1-1.

When Cate knocked at the door, Laurie hollered for her to come in. When Cate found Laurie, she quickly called the emergency number. Laurie told her friend where to find Steve's flight schedule and a list of phone numbers to try—anything to get him home.

Within minutes, skilled emergency responders surrounded Laurie. Her initial sense of relief gave way to panic as the EMTs strapped her to a backboard so they could carry her down two flights of narrow, twisting steps. Her Victorian dream transformed into a nightmare for those five steep minutes. When the EMTs asked Laurie which hospital she used, on instinct she told them Brigham and Women's Hospital in Boston, rather than the small community hospital down the street.

In the meantime, Cate reached the airline, which got a message to Steve in the cockpit as he approached Logan International Airport. Cate picked him up when he landed, and Steve was at Laurie's side within hours of her first call for help.

A cold wave of shock washed over Laurie when the doctor told her that she should have died that morning due to a brain aneurysm. If she had gone to the local hospital, they never would have had a neurosurgeon on staff with the expertise to pull her through.

The doctor described Laurie's treatment plan. First Laurie would spend a month in a rehab hospital to heal from the brain bleed. Then she would have a tricky procedure called an embolization, followed by another surgery ten days later. During the embolization, doctors would thread a catheter through the femoral (thigh) artery up into her brain to "glue" the affected cranial arteries so she would not bleed out during the subsequent surgery. The doctor told her she would have to be awake during the procedure so they could ask her questions and map out her brain activity for the neurosurgeon.

The thought of lying on the operating table, completely immobilized, yet mostly awake and aware of what was happening, frightened Laurie. But the doctor made it clear: this was the only possible plan of action. His military-like decision making and planning assured her that he knew what he was doing. She could trust him.

The embolization procedure was nearly as bad as Laurie had anticipated. She felt waves of panic as the medical staff put the catheter in, read her brain waves, and applied the medication to her brain. The room was full of medical professionals and students watching the procedure for her rare condition. The doctors asked Laurie to do simple arithmetic. They asked her to repeat short phrases. But other than these questions that helped map her brain, no one spoke to her. No one calmed or comforted her. It was all so clinical. Didn't they understand how unnerving it was?

As difficult as the embolization was to endure, the most challenging part was yet to come.

Immediately following the procedure, Laurie was moved to the recovery room. There were no available beds, so she remained on the narrow gurney and was given strict instructions not to move for the next twenty-four hours. If she moved, she might throw a clot, which could result in death or permanent paralysis.

Panic engulfed her.

Not only could she not move, she felt like an afterthought in the recovery room. The staff bustled around, but paid little attention to her. The bright lights and white walls tortured her eyes; she yearned for dim quiet. When she closed her eyes, the smell of antiseptic intensified. She wore only a hospital gown with one thin sheet over her; her body grew cold and rigid with cramped muscles on the narrow gurney. She was thirsty but couldn't drink, and no one thought to moisten her lips;

only catheters and IVs kept the fluids moving through her. Her husband was not allowed in the recovery room.

What's going on here? I know I have to hold still, but isn't anyone going to look out for me? Is this how they treat all their patients? Aren't they even going to bring me a blanket? I should be treated better than this! Why is no one paying attention to me? What if something happens and no one notices? What if I never see Steve again?

Eventually a hospital counselor came to speak with Laurie. Not only was her voice reassuring, but she offered a visualization technique that helped Laurie bear the long hours ahead. The counselor suggested revisiting an extremely pleasant experience full of sensory richness. Laurie remembered a glorious trip to San Juan, Puerto Rico, with her husband. She felt the warmth of the sun, the sand in her toes, and the lull of the water. She remembered dancing with Steve on the beach. In the ongoing strength of that memory, comfort outweighed panic, and Laurie began to sense a level of acceptance.

Laurie survived what seemed like an unending twenty-four hours.

And then she had to repeat the whole process the next day.

The brain surgery itself was not nearly as torturous as that time on the embolization gurney. After a long course of rehabilitation, Laurie regained the ability to walk, to work, and to provide comfort to others. She now works as a geriatric case manager, assisting seniors and their caregivers not only with practical plans for safety and wellbeing, but also noting the importance of those smaller things that make life more comfortable and calm.

Laurie seeks to bring to other people the same comfort she found, or hoped for, during those twenty-four hours of stillness.

COMFORT SUMMARY

Comfort is a state of physical or emotional ease. On our Vehicle of Life it is one of the tires that (when inflated) provides stability and a smooth ride. Comfort allows us some separation from crisis, at least for a moment, so that we can rest and refocus before continuing.

What brings us each comfort is personal and depends on our individual life experiences. We may find comfort in physical things, in emotional bonds, or in particular activities. Rituals and traditions are two major sources of comfort in crisis, as they reinforce normalcy, connection, and continuity.

In our culture, we often have trouble talking about comfort, sometimes from a fear of appearing narcissistic or self-indulgent. When helping others in crisis, we may need to help them name the pain before they can identify what they need for comfort. Ask questions, pay attention to verbal and physical cues, and offer new ideas when you have permission. Recognize also the need to help family members and professional personnel align their actions with the needs and wants of the person in crisis.

Control:
Power to Manage Your Life

Ironing is comfort. It's control. I'm a nutty person who likes to make sure everything is in its place. —Sandra Bullock

In the midst of writing this book, a colleague approached me about very quickly submitting a proposal for a government contract. There was no guarantee of success, but I weighed the possible upside and decided it was worth the effort. For about twelve hours, the proposal took a huge amount of my focus.

As I began working on the proposal, my air conditioning started to sputter. I called the AC maintenance company, anticipating a bill of $200 or $300 for the maintenance and whatever small parts might be needed.

I had a bigger problem than I thought. Not only did the air conditioning need more than simple maintenance, I had a humidity problem under the house that was causing rotting. The minimum to fix the AC was $600. The *real* fix totaled nearly $13,000! Shock!

I immediately started cursing my newly-ex-husband under my breath. *You dirty rat, leaving me to deal with this decrepit old house.*

STOP! Let's talk about Control, and then dissect what's happening here.

WHAT DO WE MEAN BY *CONTROL*?

Merriam-Webster defines *control* as:

1. The power to make decisions about how something is managed or done, or
2. The ability to direct the actions of someone or something.

As humans we want to exert control over many aspects of life: how we look, how we make decisions, how we use our money and resources. We like to have control over our time and energy, other people's perceptions of us, how things go at home and in the community, how our children grow up and behave. We want people with any sort of tie to our name—spouse, child, family or colleague—to act above reproach. We are embarrassed if they do something foolish, illegal, immoral, or unethical; we see their behavior as a reflection on us.

> *Crisis all but eliminates a sense of control—sometimes for only a moment, but sometimes indefinitely.*

How many of these things do we really control? Some, certainly. But for many, control is illusive rather than real. In crisis, the illusive and elusive nature of control becomes even more pronounced. Crisis all but eliminates a sense of control—sometimes for only a moment, but sometimes indefinitely.

The Value of Control

Control is important any time, but the need for it is heightened after a crisis. Control allows us to stabilize. It confers a sense of safety. (Remember the statement "I don't want to be afraid"?) It rebuilds a sense that life goes on even with all the disruptions around us.

Crisis shakes our trust that life will ever be normal again. While logic would say, "This situation is temporary," crisis cries, "No, it isn't!" In a flash our normal trust in ourselves, others, and whatever grounds us in life seems to disappear. Ironically, as soon as we reinstate one small aspect of normal life, that act triggers the confidence to attempt another, and another; and so it goes until the hope of returning stability outweighs the fear of perpetual disruption.

My dad served in the US Army in WWII, stationed in London when German bombs pounded the city. When the air raid sirens went off, Dad watched the Londoners, about to have their neighborhoods leveled, grab their teapots and run for the bomb shelters. In a terrible situation, that was one small thing they could control. Somehow or other, at four o'clock every day, they were going to have tea. Regardless of enemy bombs, these sturdy folks were determined to maintain a bit of sanity through the comfort of a "cuppa."

How We React to a Lack of Control

Visualize a Slinky®, with its circling coils. When life is going well, we are in control and the Slinky tumbles in an orderly fashion down the stairs. When we're in a crisis, instead of remaining loose and free-flowing, the Slinky's coils scrunch in on top of each other, twist, and may even lock up. We knot up like that Slinky when different parts of life feel simultaneously out of control.

Now to dissect my mild crisis...

When my colleague approached me about the government proposal, I weighed the options and made a choice. I was in control of whether or not to participate. I was *not* in control of the timeframe—it was now or never.

I *thought* I was in control when I called the air conditioning company to come at a time that was convenient for me. I *thought* I knew what to expect for a bill. But as life shows us daily, expect the unexpected. Whether I wanted it to or not, my massive air conditioning estimate came at the same time I was trying to focus on my proposal. I no longer had my pristine, controlled, vacuum of life. My proposal urgency had been compounded by my AC emergency.

Both of my "emergencies" were mild—no one suffered a serious injury, my house wasn't wrecked—but dramatic or mundane, combined crises fuel the fear that everything is spinning out of control.

Crises can trigger an emotional ripple effect. Notice my immediate reaction upon hearing the repair estimate: "Stupid ex-husband leaving me with this old house!" Where did *that* come from? I thought I had moved beyond the strong emotions of divorce. In fact, in our settlement, I had *asked* for the house due to its proximity to my mother. (And, I really should add, my ex-husband has been and continues to be extremely gracious, offering his assistance with various house projects.) While I certainly didn't expect a massive air conditioning bill, I had the resources to pay for the most immediate repair. I wasn't out on the street.

> *A crisis can unleash unexpected emotions.*

Whether self-imposed or out of the blue, dramatic or mundane, crisis has a sneaky way of unleashing an array of emotions within us, most of them connected to our fear that we will never be able to make everything OK again.

The end of the story: I got my portion of the proposal done, and I felt good about it. Regardless of the outcome, the process benefited me by forcing me to pull together certain materials that I could reuse in the future. And the AC returned to a healthy state thanks to a capable repairman and some helpful suggestions from my former husband.

But what about more severe crises?

Mild crises like mine (a.k.a. "difficulties") cause anxiety and emotional reactions. More severe crises bring more severe reactions. When a tragedy such as a deadly car accident occurs, those affected immediately may feel they are in a bad dream and wonder when they will wake up. They think "Maybe my loved ones escaped to the ditch on the side of the road and just haven't been found yet. They'll walk through the door any minute now." Eventually this "magical thinking" (as

Joan Didion calls it), this *attempt to control what happened*, ceases; reality sets in. We realize that our loved ones are not in front of us, and the next time we see them—*if* we get to see them—they will not be alive.

Similarly in divorce, I realize I may see my husband again, but he will never be *my husband* again. Whether a divorce was due to an argument, an infidelity, or simply growing apart, when the realization hits that there's no going back, a second layer of shock encompasses us.

On top of the initial shock (a car accident, divorce) and the subsequent shock (realization someone is truly gone, recognition of what divorce really means), we have to deal with whatever other changes and challenges life has in store. The instigating crisis can turn into another and another, depending on the severity of the situation. So we are back to our twisted-up Slinky. Severe crises often require multiple forms of supportive intervention, potentially over a long period of time, for new avenues of control to emerge.

Signs to Seek Professional Help

We've talked about normal reactions to crisis. Sometimes those reactions can go on too long and cause serious harm. Please talk to a mental health professional if the following symptoms continue for four to six months after the initial crisis:

- Inability to stop crying or control intense emotions such as anger, fear, or irritability
- Extreme disruption in sleep patterns; can't sleep, can't stay awake
- Lethargy and inability to bathe, dress, or maintain normal daily activities
- Inability to accept that a change has occurred (death, divorce, financial loss, destruction of home or community); expectation that the situation will return to a previous state
- Inability to discuss anything *except* the traumatic situation
- Feelings of worthlessness and self-blame for the entire crisis
- Wishing to have died from the crisis, or along with a loved one
- Inability to eat, or inability to stop eating
- Isolation from others, or feeling afraid to be alone at any time

Avoiding Talk of Control

Control shares many similarities with Comfort, including our tendency to avoid talking about it. We don't speak about comfort and control because, in general, our society reinforces the notion that good people (such as ourselves), don't actively seek them (but, really, we do). People who obviously pursue comfort are seen as narcissistic and selfish. People who are clear that control is important to them are labeled "control freak" or "domineering." We forget that there is also a *healthy* understanding of these words. (By comparison, as we'll see later, we articulate much more clearly our need for Community and Connection.)

Does this sound familiar?

"What do you want for dinner?"

"I don't know. What do you want for dinner?"

"Doesn't matter to me. You choose."

"How about Indian?"

Indian? She knows I don't like Indian. Why would she suggest Indian?

Suddenly "I don't care" turns into "I guess I do care"—in other words, "I guess I do want some control." Until we can talk about Comfort and Control in a healthy way, those rules about not being selfish or domineering have hold of us.

Control Is Personal

Some people have lives they find completely normal, but that others would think regimented and boring. Others live with a degree of...shall we say..."flexibility" that they find comfortable, but that others might find utterly chaotic. "Normal"—and control of normalcy—is a personal definition.

However we came to our control preferences, whatever nature/nurture combo influenced us, almost no one likes to feel out of control (with the possible exception of extreme sports enthusiasts!). What sends us into that sensation of being out of control is likewise personal. It may be big or small, a crisis or an irritation. It may even be undefinable—simply a nagging feeling we have.

Control (or lack thereof) is also specific to our situation. Not only can an inciting incident cause loss of control, but its implications may as well. For example, Jane is normally healthy, strong, and physically stable, but she fell and sprained her ankle. It's uncomfortable and inconvenient, but she will heal fairly quickly and, since she had no plans to run a marathon anytime soon, it's not tragic.

Jan, on the other hand, is somewhat fragile; she is diabetic and has mobility challenges. She also fell and sprained her ankle, but the event threw her far out of control. The sprain further affected her mobility, making it difficult to get exercise, so her blood sugar went up. She ended up at the doctor not only once for her sprain, but a second time for an adjustment to her diabetes medication.

As personal as control is, and as individual as our preferences for it are, of all the discomforts crisis brings, lack of control is one of the most significant. It can be as much or even more uncomfortable than physical pain.

> *Lack of control may be the most painful part of a crisis.*

Control May Appear Illogical

Because the need for control is so personal, sometimes decisions made by a person in crisis appear illogical to outsiders. In fact, sometimes the trickiest crisis interactions involve "hidden logic." There could be a few things at play.

❖ We may hold values that are outside the "norm." While those values might not be so obvious in everyday life, crisis tends to bring them to the surface.

❖ When crisis rips away things we normally control, we grasp tightly onto anything that remains.

❖ We often react strongly in crisis, so our actions to control things become exaggerated. (Remember we talked earlier about crisis bringing out extremes.)

Example: Ignacio sat across the table from his soon-to-be-ex-wife, Olivia. As their attorneys went down the list of assets, he kept mostly quiet, nodding his head or murmuring a response when needed. When they got to the beach house, he finally spoke up. "She can have it." The other three at the table looked surprised, especially when he didn't ask for any concessions in return.

Afterward, Ignacio's lawyer asked why he'd given up the house. "I'd normally suggest selling it and splitting the equity," the lawyer said, "or at least getting something from your wife in exchange."

Ignacio just shook his head. "That beach house has too many memories. Plus, it takes a beating every time there's a hurricane. I will sleep better at night if I don't have to worry about it."

> The heart has its reasons, which Reason does not know. —Blaise Pascal

Example: When Latoya got laid off from the auto factory, she got two weeks' severance pay. Almost ten years with her nose to the grindstone, and that was it. She wasn't the only one. Most of her friends worked at the plant too, and found themselves in the same pickle: no income, little savings, few job prospects in sight. So when Latoya told her girlfriends she was still taking her kids to Disneyland, they shook their heads. Any sane woman would cancel that trip and put those nickels and dimes right back in the piggybank.

When Latoya's pastor asked her what she was thinking, she said, "Brother Jones, I promised my kids we were going to Disney; come hell or high water, we are going to Disney."

Example: Peggy sighed as she watched her ninety-year-old mother eat tomato soup with croutons and marshmallows on top. It was nine o'clock at night and Peggy knew her mother would be up until 2 a.m. reading in bed. She'd tried to talk her mother into moving to a retirement community. "Think of the people you could make friends with," Peggy said. "I don't like old people!" her mother responded. "They'd cook all your meals for you," Peggy said. "They don't make food I like—and I don't want to eat dinner at five o'clock!"

Peggy sighed again. Her mother controlled few things in life, but those she did, she controlled with a vengeance.

Decisions and actions may look illogical from the outside, but to the person making them, they make perfect sense— because *she* is in control.

REGAINING CONTROL

If Control (in the positive sense) is so important, what can we do to regain it during or after a crisis? The biggest thing we can do is create normalcy, however each of us defines it.

Reconstitute Daily Habits

In the Comfort chapter we talked about how consciously incorporating rituals and traditions into (or back into) our lives comforts us. We noted that habits are similarly repetitive activities we undertake, often without paying much attention to them. To regain control, reconstituting interrupted habits helps us feel like we're running on track.

When someone is seriously ill or injured, family members often spend every spare minute at the hospital. Sometimes they forget to do routine things like brush their

> *The biggest thing we can do to regain control is create normalcy, however each of us defines it.*

teeth. They don't run home to take a shower or change into fresh clothes. One day slides into another while they stay glued to the chair waiting for a chance to go into the ICU or talk to the doctor when she is making rounds. Anxious visitors grab junk food whenever their nervous stomachs allow them to eat. And work? Who can think about work when sitting in the ICU? Any semblance of normalcy disappears.

In a time of crisis, if you slip into ignoring daily hygiene, healthful eating, or regular exercise, pay attention to this self-defeating pattern. Those behaviors can make you feel even more out of control. Take a hot shower, eat a nutritious meal, or take a short walk. Then congratulate yourself for the tangible action you have taken to restore order to your life.

Do those activities seem trivial?

During a harrowing time in my life I scheduled an appointment with a well-respected therapist. After patiently listening to my tale of woe, he looked at me from head to foot and said, "I see you have your clothes on, and they're facing in the right direction."

Was this man a creep, talking about my clothes being on? Confused, I mumbled, "Of course," not sure what was coming next.

Then he gently continued, "Becky, based on everything you're going through, if you can just get your clothes on with all of them facing the right way every day, you're doing great. Anything beyond that is a bonus."

His insight helped me appreciate the significance of mundane activities when crisis rules the day.

In a time of crisis, give yourself credit for noticing and completing even small tasks. Regardless of the type of crisis, there are specific actions you can take.

Example: You lost your job and struggle to get started each morning.

- ❖ Make a list of your priorities for the day (for example, three phone calls, one networking event, requesting two LinkedIn recommendations).
- ❖ Note the follow-up calls or emails you will make the next day based on the networking event you attended.
- ❖ Check off each item when you complete it. Checkmarks bring a sense of order and control. This builds momentum and enhances stability.

Example: You just divorced and feel overwhelmed by new responsibilities.

- ❖ List three responsibilities you already handle well.
- ❖ Think about why you handle them without difficulty.
- ❖ List one new responsibility. Consider how it is similar to the things you are already doing effectively. Use that information when you have to handle the new task.

Remember that even if you can handle only one of these ideas, you are still pumping up the tire we labeled Control on your Vehicle of Life.

Identify Small Things to Control

If I have control over a few small, even trivial, things, I find I can handle larger issues better. For example, my neighborhood tends to lose power in storms. We have big old trees from which limbs drop, and we tend to get our power restored last. Many storms ago, I figured out that if I can't get coffee in morning, at home or at a coffee shop, it really plays with me. And it's more than just the caffeine. There is just...*something*... about coffee in the morning (I know many of you understand what I mean!).

Well, clever thing that I am (when I have caffeine), I realized I could use the propane side burner on the grill to make coffee. So I got a pot that fit, and now any time there's a storm coming, I stock up on propane and powdered creamer. I don't care *what* hurricane hits, I'm going to get my coffee.

It's amazing the big things we can tolerate—if we can control a few little things.

QUESTIONS FOR REFLECTION

What's my "coffee"?

What do I have to do to make the "coffeepot" work?

Break Big Tasks into Small Pieces

When we are in crisis, normal tasks may suddenly seem overwhelming, but they still have to get done. Bills still have to be paid. Reports still have to be written.

Try breaking big tasks into manageable pieces. Some ways to do this:

❖ Set a timer and work on the task for ten minutes. When you're done, if you feel up to it, set the timer for another ten minutes; otherwise, do another ten minutes in an hour, or later in the day.

❖ Determine a certain number of items to be completed. Stop when you finish them. For example, if you have fifteen bills to pay, focus on paying five bills, and then take a break.

You may find that once you get started on a small chunk of work, you gain energy for the rest of it.

Ignore Things That Can Be Ignored

Sometimes in crisis, we realize what the truly important things are. And we realize some things that we normally do because we "should" are simply not that important. What will happen if we just stop doing them? I promise, you don't have to dust the house or wash the car as often as usual. You might even be able to skip the weekly staff meeting once in a while.

Ask For and Accept Help

When possible, ask for help with activities that don't require your participation or that you don't feel qualified to do alone. If a friend offers to pick up the kids from piano lessons, let him. If hiring someone to clean house every other week frees up your time to focus on a family member in the hospital, do it. If you can't make heads or tails of the hospital bill, find someone who can help you decipher it.

While it may feel like relinquishing control, consider that by asking for help you are maintaining the highest level of control—focusing your time and energy on the crisis at hand. Sometimes we feel guilty because we can't do it all. The goal is not to do everything yourself; the goal is to make sure the important things get done.

QUESTIONS FOR REFLECTION

What is my pattern of asking for help? Do I? Don't I? When?

What's my comfort level with accepting help?

Would I prefer to pay for help or recruit volunteers?

What are the best- and worst-case scenarios if I go it alone?

If I don't get help, who will this affect?

Right now, what do I need help with the most?

HELPING SOMEONE ELSE REGAIN CONTROL

Thelma looked like a stereotypical little old lady, but she was not as predictable as she appeared. Thelma had always been very much in control of her life. She was an African American businesswoman when few women followed that path. In the 1940s she set up a beauty salon in her home, and later she started a beautician training program. Her goal was to help other black women earn money "and not be beholden to their men."

She maintained a pristine home, inside and out, long after her husband passed away. By the time I met Thelma, she was almost bedfast and could not tolerate much food, so her kitchen held cases of Ensure® instead of groceries.

One day as we described favorite memory after favorite memory, Thelma said, "What I really miss more than anything is a hotdog all the way. I wish I could have one again."

Considering her current circumstances, I thought she was crazy. "That sounds nice," I said rather lamely.

Later, on a whim, I asked her nurse if Thelma could have a hotdog. The nurse said, "If she wants it, that's fine."

At our next visit, I asked Thelma if she'd like to try having a hotdog again. Thelma almost shouted, "Yes! Absolutely!" The plan was set. The following week, I would bring hotdogs for both of us.

When I arrived, not only was Thelma ready to eat, but she had set her table with placemats, her favorite plates, and double napkins (a necessity for hotdogs). She had even poured our drinks. Now it was time to start in on the hotdogs.

She finished hers in no time. "You know," she said, "that was a pretty good hotdog. Where did you get it?"

When I told her, she nodded and said, "Well, on your next visit, I would rather you go to Snoopy's. I like their hotdogs better."

I was flabbergasted. *Another hotdog? From a different place?* So, I checked with Thelma's nurse to see if we dared rerun the hotdog experiment and got her nod of approval. If she can handle this one, she can handle it again.

Two weeks later I stopped at Snoopy's, picked up hotdogs, and returned to Thelma's. Again, everything was ready—and she got the hotdog *the way she wanted it*.

She smiled and said, "You know, that was really good. I don't think I want another one, but it was exactly what I wanted, and it tasted just as good as I thought it was going to." Thelma had achieved that glorious melding of Comfort and Control—and she never asked for another hotdog.

When we want to help someone regain control after a shock, we don't always get a clear signal like the one Thelma gave me. Here are some suggestions for what to do and what not to do.

What to DO

Sometimes we intend to support a person in crisis, but we stumble getting started. To begin, think about the basic needs of life and relationships. Focus on taking consistent, concrete actions that are aligned with that person's situation.

DO: Offer Practical Help

When I was in seminary, back when ninety-eight percent of the students were male, I remember the professor looking up and saying to the class, "Now, gentlemen, your sermons are important, and your hospital visitations are important, but probably the most important thing in a time of crisis is your wife's casserole." There's definitely some truth to that!

When we offer practical things to a person in crisis, without being asked, we help create a safety net. A circus safety net jiggles when the trapeze artists fall into it—for good reason. The performers don't want to fall on hard ground; they need some buoyancy. In essence, that's what we do for each other—

create buoyancy for someone who can't do for himself in a time of crisis. So go ahead and take a casserole.

What are other ways to offer practical assistance? How about taking the trash to curb the night before garbage day? See if you can help shuttle the kids to the orthodontist or soccer practice. Mow the lawn. Ask if you can wash the car or get the oil changed. (See the Resources chapter for more ideas.)

At work, find a way to divvy up the affected person's responsibilities for a period of time. Offer reassurance that you won't let the Acme Project fall through. Depending on your employer's policies, you may be able to donate vacation time or paid time off (PTO) to another employee.

Crises often have financial implications. If the neighbor's teen runs away from home, not only will it impact her at work (her mental focus is not there), but she might have new expenses, such as hiring an investigator or traveling out of town. One way to assist may be to organize a financial relief effort.

Each of these items is an extension of bringing a casserole. Ultimately we need to feed the significant need at the moment. Remember, when in crisis, we often lose the physical, mental, and emotional capability to get normal life activities done. Helping to keep those things running eases re-entry back into normal life. The person in crisis feels stabilized because life is now less chaotic—even if others are temporarily taking control of the details.

DO: Remember the Platinum Rule

Since we are all individuals who process crises differently, and since we all have different definitions of "control" and "normal," when offering assistance to those in crisis, it behooves us to understand their perspective. You may remember the Golden Rule: Do unto others as you would have them do unto you. More important may be the Platinum Rule (from Dr. Tony Alessandra): Do unto others *as they want to be done unto.*

Initially with Thelma, I took charge and got hotdogs without asking her preference. While the first attempt created an OK experience, something was lacking. Thelma really needed to direct the whole process. When she did, it made all the difference.

In crisis, we need to understand a person's pre-crisis "normal." It may not match our "normal." We can get into trouble when we try to impose our definition, so we have to make sure we use the right lens to observe the situation. Sometimes loving, generous gifts are rebuffed ("I did

> We need to understand a person's pre-crisis "normal," which may be different from our own normal.

something really nice—I got her hotdogs!—and she wasn't grateful"). Rejection may be one method people use to regain control, especially if we try to force something on them that they don't value.

DO: Model Normalcy

Stability and control often take a major hit during prolonged or chronic crisis situations. As a caregiver or co-worker, you can serve as a valuable resource by gently leading, prompting, or modeling those habits that create better health—whether work health, physical health, or emotional health. This form of help guides a crisis-affected person back to a place where he can control a normal aspect of life, even if it is just that one little part.

For example, your co-worker may skip lunch or rarely take a break because he's trying to catch up on work missed while caring for a chronically ill child. You might invite him to join you for a ten-minute walk outside, or to enjoy a healthy snack in the break room. These bits of exercise, good food, and pleasant company not only provide mental stimulation, but also nudge him toward simple ways to maintain normal health routines, even during high stress times.

DO: Offer Space to Gain Perspective

When my daughter Laurie was in middle school, she bumped up against perfectionist anxiety on a regular basis. As she was going to bed one night, she'd gotten herself tied up in knots. I saw she was about to spin out of control, and I had a flash of wisdom.

I said, "Laurie, normally Mom wants you to tell the truth about everything, but tomorrow morning, you and I are going to do things a little differently. Tomorrow morning I want you to tell me that you have a really, really bad stomachache. Anna will go to school, but you and I are going to stay home."

"OK," she said, eyes wide. "If you say so."

The next morning she playacted like a pro, doubled over in "pain," and I sent Anna off to school by herself. I tucked Laurie back into bed. While she slept in, I went to the video store and rented two funny videotapes.

Laurie and I spent a good chunk of the day watching movies and eating Girl Scout Peanut Butter Patties® with milk. And we talked about "stuff." Before Anna came home from school, we hid the evidence. By then, Laurie felt better and was ready to go back to school the next day.

I thought letting Laurie stay home was a good thing to do, a smart thing to do. It helped her calm down, be silly, talk about what was bothering her, put things in perspective. But years later, I found out from Laurie that letting her stay home to get her middle-school self back into control was one of the most loving, healing things I ever did for her.

> *Giving someone space to gain perspective can be emotional oxygen.*

Sometimes you have to do something illogical—odd, light, fluffy, humorous—to turn a tense, agitated situation into a calm, controlled one. Taking an unusual approach can be dicey, so you need to know the person well, but when it works and that space is created, it can be emotional oxygen.

DO: Remember Who Is Really In Control

Joanne epitomized the image of a "Southern lady." Raised with her sister in a small North Carolina town, Joanne had the homemaking skills of her mother and the hospitable personality of her father. Gracious, headstrong, and forthright, Joanne welcomed the hospice team into the tiny apartment she and her sister, Grace, adorned with family treasures.

Equally protective of each other, the sisters filled our visits with pleasant chitchat focused on old family stories, cards from distant relatives, and descriptions of casseroles dropped off by thoughtful neighbors. Joanne and Grace both deflected my regular attempts to steer the conversation onto weightier matters.

The guiding principles of hospice care include honoring the decisions made by the patients and their families. Those principles involve conversations some people find unpleasant. Does the patient want a do-not-resuscitate order? Is there a funeral plan in place? And so on. No one on our hospice team had made any progress initiating these conversations with Joanne and Grace.

The social worker and I decided that these loving sisters must be protecting each other from a potentially distressing conversation. If offered privacy, surely they would want to share their wishes related to Joanne's care. Not wimps at all, both of these women had charted their course through life for many years. They just needed the right setting to do that now—and we would make that happen.

Knowing the apartment was too small for two private conversations to take place at once, the social worker and I "just happened" to show up simultaneously for a visit. The social worker offered to take Grace out for coffee. Fortunately, Grace accepted the invitation. The stage was set. Now Joanne and I could *really* talk.

Before I could begin my first well-rehearsed sentence, Joanne proclaimed, "I've been thinking about my sweet Papa and the important things he taught me. You know, dear, his favorite expression, and the rule that's guided my life, is 'Always look on the sunny side.' He was right. I've spent my life talking about just happy things and somehow everything has worked out fine. Now, what is it you'd like to talk about today?"

So much for my plan.

I wanted Joanne to have control over her end-of-life choices. Joanne wanted control of what would and would not be discussed. That was the *only* important choice to Joanne.

The social worker reported a similar conversation with Grace. Papa's philosophy prevailed.

Joanne outlived her prognosis by nine months, and we always kept our conversations "on the sunny side."

What NOT to Do

When helping someone regain control, our good intentions can lead to not-so-good results. Here are some actions to avoid.

DON'T: Do Nothing

Think of how many times you've heard someone say, "I didn't go because I didn't want to do the wrong thing" or "I didn't call because I didn't want to say the wrong thing." While saying nothing may at times be better than saying something stupid, I would guess that when we make statements like these, we're trying to exert a sense of control *for ourselves*.

If you're not ready to talk directly to the person in crisis, start with sending a card or note. Regardless of the situation, people almost always want to know you are thinking about them. You could even include a gift card for coffee, groceries, or gasoline.

If you want to see the person but don't know what to say, take something that will be an icebreaker. Beautiful flowers, a memento from a cherished sports team, or a CD of favorite music will take the focus off your opening sentence.

DON'T: Offer Platitudes

As humans, we have a core need to make sense of things that don't make sense. As a result we may say things we think are kind and will help bring the situation back into control, but they end up being hurtful.

These platitudes often come out through religious statements: "This is part of God's plan" or "God needed him in Heaven" or "God's creating a great test here." All kinds of things get laid onto God during a time of crisis. (God can handle it. That's not the point.)

The first problem is, not everyone is religious. Injecting God into the situation may only make it worse and could potentially fracture your relationship. The second problem is, even religious folks may not find this kind of statement helpful. (If, on the other hand, someone in crisis makes this type of statement, don't argue.)

The other platitude we often say is "I'm sure it will be better tomorrow." Again, a well-intended statement, but you actually can't be sure that it *will* be better tomorrow. It may *never* be better. This is the kind of statement that makes the *person who's saying it* feel better. It's reassuring to the speaker, and she believes she's said something kind.

Instead, when people need reassurance (which is a big part of Control), simply let them know you are sorry something happened, you share their frustration over difficult circumstances, and you believe in them.

DON'T: Make Comparisons

It's OK to let people in crisis know we empathize with them, but it is *not* OK to say "I know what you feel." As many times as we're told not to, we still find ourselves saying it. We *may* have a *sense* of what people are going through, but we are *not* inside their heads or their hearts, so we *cannot* possibly know what they feel.

And by all means, avoid competitive grief. Some sympathizers try to compare their own situation (perhaps again exerting control for themselves). To commiserate is one thing, to compete another. It doesn't work.

DON'T: Offer Ambiguous "Help"

Another thing we often say with graciousness and good intent is "Just call me if you need something." People tell me that when they hear "just call me" without any clue to the type of help being offered, they start to feel an extra burden of responsibility.

This well-intended offer forces someone, in the very midst of a crisis, to use those faculties most challenged by the crisis. Unless some need is burningly obvious ("Call an ambulance!"), most people have trouble thinking, focusing, concentrating, listing things in order, prioritizing, and even just remembering!

If you want to offer help, try offering something specific. "May I get you a glass of water?" "Shall I pick up the kids from school today?" "How about I pick up a few things at the grocery store for you?"

DON'T: Smother with Care

One day I was visiting Haruko, who had to come to grips with her son's terminal illness. We'd talked for a short time about him, his impending death, what it meant to her, things that helped her cope. I opened my mouth to make a "Chaplain Becky" statement, and Haruko put up her hand: "I've been cared for as much as I can handle today. I just need to be by myself now."

I realized that ten to fifteen minutes was all she could take; whatever else she needed to do, she needed to do it by herself.

Sometimes we help people regain control simply by getting out of their way. Even when we have good intentions, good training, and good skills, people may need us only a little; then they want and *need* to be on their own.

At one end of the caring spectrum is neglect; at the other end, which we sometimes forget, is overcaring, a.k.a. "smothering." We need

> *Sometimes we help people regain control simply by getting out of their way.*

to make sure we are offering what the person in crisis needs, not what *we* need. (Remember, the definition of Control is personal.)

HIGHLIGHT STORY: ROBERTA'S PRISON

Roberta Jenkins was in her fifties and had Lou Gehrig's disease. She had become paralyzed; she had no ability to speak or to move from the neck down. But Roberta was still alive inside. Her eyes flashed with understanding, and her mouth curled with a smile. She was aware of everything going on around her, but, in all honesty, visiting her tested me. The conversation I might normally have with people became a monolog (and I'm no Johnny Carson).

Roberta's husband, Ray, attended to her in every possible way. He actively sought out all the developing technology that might help her communicate, such as gadgets to translate her electrical system into sound through the computer. None of it worked, but he never gave up trying.

One day Ray came running into the room, extremely excited. He held something in his hand. It looked like a rough-hewn crown. He ran over and put it on Roberta's head, shouting, "You've gotta see! You've gotta see!"

I couldn't imagine anything more peculiar. And then Ray pushed something on the top of the crown, ran down to the foot of the bed, and held up a board that had rows of letters on it. All of a sudden I realized that on top of Roberta's "crown" sat a laser pointer.

Ever so slowly, Roberta moved her head and pointed to letters. Suddenly I began to track what she was spelling. I sat there as she spelled little by little, tiny motion by tiny motion, "I-h-a-v-e..." She continued slowly letter by letter to spell out "I have come out of prison."

In that moment, I realized that no other piece of control was as important to Roberta as the control of her communication. By the arduous work of nodding her head precisely enough to point the beam at letters, Roberta taught me about our completely innate, intrinsic quest to communicate and to have control over *something* in our lives.

Over the next six months, in this manner Roberta dictated letters to friends to whom she had not been able to write in years. She left stories for her grandchildren. She even left part of the history of the women's group at her church.

This new form of communication also allowed Roberta to share more of her true self. One day I came in and she began spelling faster than I could keep up. I made the mistake of guessing at what I thought she was saying and, being there in "chaplain" mode, I put some kind of meaning to it that was perhaps a bit serious. Roberta got a huge grin on her face and started spelling again. She looked at me a little bit frustrated, because what she spelled was "That was a joke"—and I missed it!

Then, ever so slowly, Roberta's disease robbed her of the ability to move her head, and she gradually moved back into that place of isolation. But I dare say that six-month window of time was more precious to her than any other point in her life.

CONTROL SUMMARY

Control is the power to make decisions about how something is managed or done, or the ability to direct the actions of someone or something. While we sometimes have a cultural attitude that people who seek control are "control freaks," in reality Control offers stability and a sense of safety, especially in crisis. Even a small addition of air to this tire on our Vehicle of Life can help us regain normalcy.

Like Comfort, Control is personal, based on our own life experiences. To regain control in a crisis, it helps to reconstitute daily habits, identify small things to control, break big things into small pieces, ignore things that can be ignored, and ask for and accept help.

When helping others in crisis, as with Comfort, remember the Platinum Rule ("Do unto other as *they* want to be done unto"). Understand the other person's pre-crisis "normal," and model normalcy for them. Offer practical help and space to gain perspective. Don't offer platitudes, comparisons, or ambiguous "help." Don't do nothing, and don't smother. Remember, Control is personal. Find out what the person in crisis needs to feel more safe and stable.

Community:
Sharing Your Life

No man is an island entire of itself; every man is a piece of the continent, a part of the main…
—John Donne, Meditation XVII from
Devotions upon Emergent Occasions (1623)

Twenty-six-year-old Billy's pride and joy was his pick-up truck. It was one of those big bruisers with an extended cab that could carry six people and haul a ton and a half. When Billy lost his job, he decided to be thrifty and handle some home repairs himself. Unfortunately his experience level with working on the roof did not match his zeal to save money. Billy fell coming down the ladder and fractured both of his legs. With no income or insurance he had to scramble financially to hold on to his precious truck. His small rental house had no garage, so his baby was out in the elements, and due to his physical condition, he couldn't drive or maintain it. Billy's truck symbolized everything that was going wrong in his life at that point.

Billy's friends were solid, stand-up guys, but goodness knows they weren't going to hold his hand or offer deep philosophical advice. One night as they sat at the neighborhood bar, they began talking about him.

"Too bad Billy can't be down here like he used to be, can't shoot pool with us."

"I wonder what it would be like if I were in Billy's spot?" said Cal. (Young males have the capacity for empathy, even if they wouldn't call it that.)

After further discussion, they hatched a plan.

On a beautiful spring Saturday morning they showed up at Billy's house with all the paraphernalia needed to wash and wax his truck. One of the fellows changed the oil in case it had gotten mucked up while the truck sat unused.

Billy watched from the window. Cal came in to shoot the breeze with him. They told truck stories and hunting stories and tales of the backwoods where that bulldog of a truck plowed through brush and mud.

When the crew finished their truck maintenance, Cal asked Billy what would make him happy today.

"I'd love to have a beer and go for a ride."

Cal popped a beer can for him, and Billy took a couple swigs. The guys helped Billy into his truck, and drove out to one of their favorite fishing holes. They didn't get out of the truck, but they rolled down the windows, and talked about catching fish—what kind of bait they'd use, what was biting right now, how they'd fry it up over a campfire. When Billy'd had enough, they headed home and got him back in the house.

Billy told me later, "It was the best darn day I ever had."

Those guys never had a course in counseling, philosophy, or religion 101, but they lived out every bit of it. *That* is community.

WHAT DO WE MEAN BY *COMMUNITY*?

Merriam-Webster offers many definitions for the word *community*. Several of them are relevant for our discussion:

1. A unified body of individuals,
2. Society at large,
3. A group of people who live in the same area, or
4. A group of people who have the same interests, religion, race, etc.

In some ways, we define our community the way we need to and want to. For some people, a community of one is quite sufficient (though that singular community may find it hard to fill all the needed roles in a crisis). For others, the community acts like an accordion, expanding and contracting based on what's happening in life.

The Value of Community

The value of community comes from practical things, such as casseroles and clean pick-up trucks, as well as emotional connections, such as unasked favors and truck rides in the spring. Both the practical support and the emotional support pump up the tire labeled Community on our Vehicle of Life, so we are equipped to move through a crisis.

Sometimes a small, specific, focused community can address a particular need, comfort a particular hurt, or calm a particular fear. For example, a medical community has information, resources, and treatments. Within that cluster of people we find the safety net we need to hold us in that time.

Sometimes a broader community with an extensive scope of individuals and personalities, such as a church, neighborhood, or club, gives us a feeling of wealth. When we have many friendships and connections in our bank of relationships, even if we don't call on them directly, knowing they are available buoys us. And, in an interesting way, our reliance on the community buoys it too. Most of us want to be needed. Communities are no different.

> *We need the underlying support of community, even if the community members are not physically present with us.*

A community that plays an obvious role in supporting someone in crisis feels worthwhile and affirmed. Both the person in crisis and the community assisting during crisis receive value.

John Donne's message that no man is an island becomes most poignantly clear in a crisis. There is no doubt that in crisis many of us require solitary time. But in general, we need and even crave the underlying support of community, even if the community members are not physically present with us.

As soon as he could point and click, Trey Owen played video games. He talked about games. He designed games. He dreamed of building a gaming business. Even as a working college student, he participated daily with his online group as both player and teacher. His parents were proud of his technological abilities, but it wasn't until Trey was killed in a tragic car wreck that they realized the extent of his gaming community and Trey's significance in it.

People who knew Trey only through his online presence flooded his heartbroken parents with messages of sympathy and testimonies of Trey's influence. His parents learned that Trey's knowledge and integrity had established him as a role model for other gamers, inspiring them to make good choices offline as well as on. Several of his online friends traveled cross country to attend Trey's memorial service.

The comfort Trey's friends provided the Owen family was matched only by the Owens' deep appreciation, which the gamers carried back to their community.

Types of Communities

We may be surprised by the number and types of communities we connect with during a crisis. The most common are family, friends, and faith communities, but don't overlook others.

Family – Family is the original form of community. Whether immediate family, family of origin, or extended family, they are often the first people we turn to in crisis. And indeed they often experience a crisis with us.

Friends – The word "friends" may bring to mind best friends and close friends, but I would also place in this category neighborhoods, in which we are brought together by geography, and clubs, in which the members share a common interest.

Faith – For some people, a faith community (church, synagogue, mosque, temple, etc.) is an important part of daily life. For others, it isn't. For some, it may be a low priority until crisis hits.

Workplace – Do you consider your workplace a community? Most of us spend five out of seven days with our colleagues. If that doesn't qualify as a community, I don't know what does. Most of us probably see our colleagues more often than we do our extended families. (Shoot, many of us talk to our hairdresser more often than we do our extended families.)

Specialized – Community can mean more than emotional relationships. Sometimes we need very practical and business-oriented communities. We mentioned the medical establishment as an example. Financial and legal advisors are another specialty community. We may need someone we trust and can sit with in comfort and confidence to discuss private matters, especially during a crisis.

Created – In the early 1990s I had the profound experience of ministering to a different type of "family"—the HIV/AIDS community. Much of society had judged and blamed those who had acquired HIV/AIDS. Many of those who were gay found, due to lack of acceptance by their family or religion of origin, that they had to create new communities, new families, and new relationships. As hospice personnel, we were highly embraced, because we accepted, loved, and cared for all our patients as best we could. For a variety of reasons, many of us may identify with "created" communities.

Online – At the same time we complain about "too much technology" taking us away from "real human interactions," we must recognize that the availability of the internet has offered a way for people to come together from anywhere on the planet (at this writing Facebook has about 1.4 *billion* users). And it has allowed previously dispersed and/or marginalized communities to come together. People with highly specialized interests—breeding dwarf tomatoes, traveling in Finland, managing a rare chronic disease—are able to have a community thanks to technology.

QUESTION FOR REFLECTION

What types of communities do I belong to?

INTERACTING WITH YOUR COMMUNITY

In crisis we frequently call on our valued community. Sometimes our interactions take a different form from what we expect. Whether you are the person in crisis or are walking alongside someone in crisis, you may need to expand your community, to actively manage it, or even to keep it at a distance.

Politely Managing Your Community

I visited Javier in the hospital one day. He was having a good day; his pain had subsided, and he was in a positive frame of mind. We had a lovely conversation and laughed a lot.

The next week I called to schedule another visit. His daughter Bianca very gently said, "Dad really enjoyed your visit, but I think we need to make it shorter next time because he was so exhausted after you left." Oh!

Bianca reminded me that positive, even pleasurable, events still take energy. We all know the feeling of putting on a dinner party that we thoroughly enjoy—and then dealing with the fatigue that sets in afterward. The person in crisis exerts energy as the "host" of a visit or call.

Positive, even pleasurable, events still take energy.

As **community members** around someone in crisis, it behooves us to remember that person may need to marshal his energy for more important things than conversing with us.

As members of the **inner circle**, we can help look out for that person, the way Bianca did for her dad. Whether requesting or declining assistance, inviting or limiting interaction, creating a special experience or decreasing stimulation, the people closest to the person in crisis often swing between the roles of initiator and gatekeeper. Be aware these roles also require energy; when in them, you may need to protect yourself too.

As the **person in crisis**, we must recognize that is it OK to politely control our community. We do not have to expend our emotional and physical energy by taking care of everyone else. (This applies in non-medical as well as medical crises.)

Some examples of polite control:

❖ Yolanda was blessed with an abundance of attention from her church. Her family posted a sign on her hospital door: "Yolanda would love to see you, but is too tired. Please send cards for now so she can enjoy them when she has energy."

❖ Jack had many supportive colleagues. His wife posted the following sign: "Jack would love to see you one at a time. Please call Louise to schedule a visit at 2 p.m. on the next available day."

❖ Martha's husband sent the following email: "Martha naps frequently. To avoid disturbing her, please call her cell phone instead of the landline. Leave a message and she will call you back when she is able. Thank you for your patience and understanding."

Crisis does not excuse rudeness, but does offer a mighty good reason to politely protect whoever needs it most.

Coordinating Your Community

William and Carol were, by personality, private people. They had a small family, both immediate and extended. They didn't belong to a faith community or any civic organizations. They were fine upstanding people who gave to charity and did wonderful things, but they were not "joiners" and chose to limit the number of people in their day-to-day life.

William's pancreatic cancer diagnosis raised new questions about their deliberately private life. Would they maintain their control, limiting the number of people coming and going? Or would they change their pattern and have strangers in their home? Many neighbors appreciated them and wanted to help in their time of crisis. What would be the best balance?

William and Carol chose to look at Community through the lenses of Comfort and Control.

❖ Comfort – What would feel best?

❖ Control – How would they manage the flow of Community coming and going in their home?

William and Carol decided on a midpoint in the extremes. They agreed to "expand the borders" around their home and increase the number of people being privy to their home life. They agreed they would be comfortable with more people than usual, but maybe not as many as some folks expected.

They made use of CaringBridge®, an online service that allowed one person to be their neighborhood go-between. The neighbors received a polite email stating that William and Carol appreciated their thoughts and support, and that if the neighbors wanted to help, some meals would be appreciated. The email explained that Wendy at 443 Oak Street would serve as the contact person and that the entire neighborhood could collaborate through CaringBridge. Wendy, in conjunction with William and Carol, set up a schedule for meals, and she delivered them personally. Periodically William and Carol asked Wendy to take a break so someone else could deliver the meals. They now felt comfortable allowing additional people to come close, but only one at a time.

By letting technology help them manage their community, William and Carol combined Comfort, Control, and Community in a way that met their needs and allowed their community members to support them. We can make difficult times more bearable for ourselves and others, but the process often requires thoughtful intention and creativity.

Varying Your Community

When we are in crisis, the community we need, want, or value can change on any given day. Does this mean we're fickle? No.

Consider: Most of us don't crave peanut butter and jelly sandwiches at every meal every day. Most of us don't want to wear a wool coat every day, especially in July.

We have no problem cooking different food each day, wearing a variety of clothes, watching different TV shows, or reading books one day and magazines another. The same can be true for the community that we need or want around us.

As a person in crisis, recognize who and what will be most helpful and encouraging for you. And as the community around that person, recognize that shifting attention does not signify diminished value of your generosity or expertise.

Situations change. Meet the current need.

Avoiding or "Protecting" Your Community

Sometimes we not only seek out different people to be part of our community in crisis, but momentarily turn our backs on people who are part of our regular community. Sometimes we avoid our community because we simply don't have the energy to expend. Other times we may avoid them out of a desire to protect them from something. We may even "replace" someone in a significant role.

For example, as a chaplain I often heard people say flat out, "I can't talk to my minister about this." They would proceed to spill their guts to me about something that was gnawing at them. It might have been fear of death and what happens after death; it might have been something they had never confessed to their priest.

In my case, I was often filling the religious leader's role, but someone may also be protecting a spouse, family members, or close friends. I've heard many times:

- ❖ "My wife would leave me if I told her how I failed."
- ❖ "I wouldn't be one of the guys anymore if they had any idea this was going on."
- ❖ "I can't let my Rotary Club know; it would worry them too much."

We want to protect our community; we don't want to make them sad, angry, or disappointed. At some point we will have to look those people in the eye, and we may not want a particular topic on the table between us. Whether we're protecting ourselves, another person, or our relationship with that person, we don't want to disclose some part of ourselves.

This dynamic gets particularly tricky in faith communities where there is an assumption that the degree to which you "suffer" is tied directly to the amount of faith you have. So, if you suffer, you yourself are to blame because you don't have a strong enough faith. In order to make ourselves feel better, and to make sure everyone in the faith community feels OK, we insist we're doing fine.

When to hold back? When to share? It's tricky. Generally speaking, my experience indicates that getting an issue out in the open tends to decrease its magnitude and make it more manageable. Whether you talk to a counselor, spiritual leader, or friend, *usually* you will feel better.

> *Getting an issue out in the open tends to decrease its magnitude and make it more manageable.*

QUESTIONS FOR REFLECTION

How do I interact with my communities during crisis?

Do I need to adjust anything about my interaction? If so, what?

Safe Strangers

Sometimes when we find ourselves protecting other people or relationships, or avoiding them because we aren't quite ready to open up, part of what is bothering us may get confessed to a "safe stranger."

Safe strangers are people who come into our lives at crisis points, when we have very particular needs. We need someone who is close to us, but not so close that she gets caught up in the drama, yet not so distant that she doesn't really give a hoot. We may need information, advice, or just a sympathetic ear during a crazy and chaotic time. We need someone level-headed, whose opinion we respect and feedback we trust.

We find ourselves quickly feeling comfortable and building bonds of trust with safe strangers. But they also have a "distance" to them. A safe stranger typically is not a spouse, family member, or friend, and may not even be our regular minister, lawyer, or therapist. A safe stranger more typically is someone like a chaplain (as I was), a special nurse, a career coach, an attorney, or a respected acquaintance.

Safe strangers can serve a crucial role in our temporary close circle of community, even if that role lasts for just one short conversation.

This type of relationship can be confusing to those around us. Spouses, family members, close friends, or colleagues may see us become incredibly close to someone in a very short period of time. They wonder why we are distancing ourselves from our normal relationships.

As a hospice chaplain, I worked with patients in their last days, weeks, or months of life. Simultaneously I was part of intense conversations with family members preparing for the death of a loved one. When the time came for the patient's funeral, family members often requested that the other hospice caregivers and I sit with them on one of the front rows, while others who had known the deceased much longer might be seated farther back. At first it felt awkward to sit in

> **SAFE STRANGERS**
> *People who come into our lives during crisis, who we quickly feel comfortable with and build trust with, but who also have a "distance" to them. We may develop an incredible bond with them during crisis, but it is rarely sustained beyond crisis.*

that place of honor since we'd entered this family's life so recently, but families insisted that they wanted us beside them for this final part of the journey. And of course there were questions when I was asked to perform part of the service along with the family's regular pastor or rabbi. How dare the family bring in a stranger at such an intimate and holy time?

I came to realize that those short-term, but highly chiseled relationships formed around crisis have a unique place in a person's life. A safe stranger often appears for a span of time within a crisis, creating an incredible bond, but that bond is rarely sustained beyond the crisis. We need to move on after a crisis, and maintaining a relationship that was formed during that time in some ways holds us there. The safe stranger allows for a sense of vulnerability that can then be closed off, compartmentalized in a unique chapter of life. Often remembered fondly, the safe stranger also moves on.

These "safe stranger" relationships are perfectly normal and healthy. It's important for the person going through the storm to realize they can call upon these new resources. It's equally important for people in the community to realize what is happening and not to feel snubbed because they take a back seat for a while. The role of safe stranger simply needs to be acknowledged and honored for what it is.

QUESTIONS FOR REFLECTION

Have I been a safe stranger for someone else? If so, in what situation?

Do I need a safe stranger to talk to in this crisis? If so, who are some options?

Opening Up Too Soon

Picture yourself with someone you don't know well, say in a job interview for another department at work. Suddenly you feel ill and—oh no!—throw up on the manager interviewing you. Now imagine what your next conversation is like. Awkward! No matter how many times the manager says, "Don't worry," "I understand," or "It's OK," future conversations may feel forever tainted with that experience. Just as with a delicate fabric, no matter how carefully you try to clean it, the experience leaves a stain.

Sometimes in a crisis, the need to unburden yourself is overwhelming. Suddenly you find yourself telling someone you just met or barely know—a neighbor who happens to stop by to hand you the newspaper that's been sitting on the sidewalk for a week—the most intimate details of your life. Afterward, you suddenly panic, wondering if she will keep your conversation confidential. Will she blab to the rest of the neighborhood? Even if she does maintain your confidence, can you ever face her again?

When making a first or second visit as a chaplain when we hadn't yet had time to develop familiarity and trust, I could predict what would happen if a patient jumped into unburdening a dark secret or a painful confession. Though the patient initially might have felt relief, and knew the information was held in absolute confidence, he would decline future visits, or there would be guardedness in ongoing conversations.

It was just a part of what happened. What do you do if someone shares too much with you too quickly?

❖ Accept the fact that words said cannot be "unsaid."

❖ Deal privately with any opinions or emotions you experience around what was shared.

❖ Do not avoid the person, but realize that the next conversation (if one takes place) may be uncomfortable.

❖ Plan ahead of time for a simple, straightforward way to acknowledge the awkwardness without dwelling on it. Here is one way to open the conversation: "I appreciate the confidence you placed in me to share your deep feelings. I am always available if you need another time like that [if that is true], but it's also OK for us to talk about other things. You decide what works best for you."

When Your Community Fails You

In Part 2 of this book, we'll discuss assumptions in more detail, but one common assumption ties to Community, especially in a time of crisis: "My family and friends will be there to support me."

When that assumption holds true, it is powerful and uplifting. It will get us through incredibly hard times. But, let's face it, people get scared, people don't always have the kind of resources they need, and sometimes people just flat wear out.

When our assumption that our community will be there for us starts to crumble, it can be debilitating. We feel abandoned, isolated, lost. We don't know where to turn.

But not only does the person in crisis feel bad, the people in the community likely feel bad as well. They may feel resentful that they are being called on to do too much. They may feel ill-equipped. They may feel guilty because they want to help but, for a variety of reasons, they can't.

Worse is when a sidewinder sneaks in the back door of your emotional house and takes you completely off guard.

Monique had been a widow for almost a year. We'd been meeting periodically for bereavement support, and she had recovered steadily. She had returned to work, explored new pastimes, and even considered new relationships.

One day I knocked on the kitchen door for our appointment. Monique didn't answer right away, but her car was parked there, so I knocked again. Eventually she opened the door.

Not only had Monique been crying, she had been *sobbing*. It took me completely off guard.

Monique thrust a crumpled paper in my face. What was this offensive document? Her husband's parking pass. Someone at his company had forgotten to take him out of the system, and the annual update was sent automatically.

That misstep ripped the scab right off Monique's healing heart, and part of her transported back to that terrible time eleven months earlier. She felt betrayed by her husband's work community. They were supposed to know better. They were supposed to take care of this.

An oversight, slip of the tongue, or computer error can take us back into a place of hurt. *Mistakes happen. We get to choose how to respond.* Unfortunately, those things happen. We're human. We make mistakes.

Sometimes the more community we have involved in our lives, the greater the chance of error.

Then we do what we need to. We decide if we have the fortitude to let it go, if we lovingly write off this part of our community, or if we set the hurt aside temporarily and say we'll look at it again later.

QUESTIONS FOR REFLECTION

Has my community failed me in some way?

If so, how am I handling it?

Having a Small Community

Some people have small communities, perhaps a few close friends or maybe even one primary person (often a spouse). Introverts sometimes fall in this category; they are often comfortable spending time alone or in very small groups.

In a crisis though, we may hit challenges when we have a small bank of relationships. We may need a level of support that overwhelms our community; its members may lack the skills, resources, information, or time required to assist us.

And if we draw on the same people for support over and over, they may feel pulled, stretched, overwhelmed, or simply worn out. They may have other things to attend to that they've neglected while offering us support. And when they pull away, they may feel frustrated, guilty, or dissatisfied with the supportive experience.

Earlier in this chapter we looked at William and Carol's decision to expand their community based on their crisis needs. By understanding how they lived their *pre*-crisis lives, we can learn several lessons that help mitigate having a small community:

❖ **Act in a manner authentic to your personality, but do so politely.** Even though they maintained a distance from their neighbors, William and Carol were always cordial and respectful.

❖ **Contribute to your community in some way.** William and Carol donated flats of flowers to neighborhood beautification projects.

❖ **Show kindness and compassion in ways that fit your personality.** Wendy, William and Carol's meal coordinator, had experienced a terrible shock three years earlier when her mother was killed in a car accident. William and Carol had made a charitable gift in honor of Wendy's mother.

❖ **Be true to your principles, but remain open to new ways to experience them.** Personal privacy was a core value for William and Carol. While they expanded their borders during crisis, they maintained privacy by appointing Wendy as their go-between.

> *People with very small communities face the biggest challenges in crisis.*

In my experience, people with very small communities face the biggest challenges in crisis. By far, those who find themselves out on a limb alone struggle even more than those who run into serious financial issues. They may find that the professionals they call on in crisis (medical or otherwise) become their default community. If they have money, they can sometimes hire a "community," i.e., pay people to help them, but that is a tough position for most of us to be in.

If you have a small community, my best advice is to start expanding it *now*. Don't wait for a crisis before you recognize the need for the support a community brings.

QUESTIONS FOR REFLECTION

Are there things I should be doing now to expand my community? If so, what?

MUTUAL REINFORCEMENT
ON THE ROAD TO RESILIENCE

Shocking times often elicit great generosity from the communities who care about us. Repeatedly, people think about us, give to us, or perhaps even sacrifice for us.

It's OK to need and accept help. Generosity creates a sense of safety and increased stability

Learning to be both a giver and a receiver builds resilience.

for the recipient. Generosity creates a sense of satisfaction and peace of mind for the giver. Learning to be both a giver and a receiver builds resilience.

Initially we may think that the community does all the giving and the person in crisis does all the receiving. But in Figure 7 notice that not only does the community give support, but the person in crisis shares something—the experience itself.

Figure 7 Giver-Receiver Positive Reinforcement Cycle

Gives support

Community   Person in Crisis

Shares experience

Sharing a crisis experience can be a gift to the community. The act of living through a challenge offers lessons and encouragement to others. The person in crisis doesn't even have to do anything extra. Simply by allowing others to observe her experience, she becomes not only a recipient but a benefactor.

Then the real magic occurs. Openly moving through the experience and strengthening the community by example *fortifies the person in crisis.*

Crisis often exposes the parts of life we shelter from public view — physical and mental illness, abuse, addiction, disability, grief — each of which exposes our vulnerability and fear of life gone wrong. When a person dealing with a shock allows the community to experience the journey with her, she shares the gift of normalizing the unknown, unfamiliar, or stigmatized.

Back in 1974 the American public did not discuss breast cancer openly. A few weeks after becoming First Lady, Betty Ford underwent a mastectomy, and then discussed her experience with candor.

"When other women have this same operation, it doesn't make any headlines," she told *Time*. "But the fact that I was the wife of the President put it in headlines and brought before the public this particular experience I was going through.

It made a lot of women realize that it could happen to them. I'm sure I've saved at least one person—maybe more." (*Time*, November 4, 1974)

Four years later, the Ford family staged an intervention, requiring Betty to get honest about her addiction to alcohol and pain medications. Once more, she invited the public along on her journey, this time to sobriety, and the American public accepted her offer. Reporters said that Betty Ford "put a face on alcoholism as a disease."

> *When a person dealing with a shock allows the community to experience the journey with her, she shares the gift of normalizing the unknown, unfamiliar, or stigmatized.*

Does the process of moving toward resilience require the platform of a First Lady of the United States of America? No.

The people who gave permission for their names and stories to be used in this book consider themselves everyday people. None is famous, wealthy, or in a position of great power. When I thanked them for allowing their stories to be used, to a person they expressed surprise that their stories were special. Each wondered, "Will my story really help somebody?"

The answer is Yes. Yes, our shared experiences *do* help pave the rocky road to resilience.

HIGHLIGHT STORY: COMMUNITY BLESSINGS

Miami, December 11, 1992. Mrs. Acuña-Rodriguez grew impatient as her car slowly snaked along in an endless line of cars. *It's not rush hour yet. Why is traffic so slow?* Then she saw the accident. *¡Dios Santo!* she thought. She began to pray for the poor soul in the crushed car.

A few hours later Mrs. Acuña-Rodriguez sat on the front porch waiting for her daughter to get home, when a neighbor rode up on his bike.

"Mrs. Acuña-Rodriguez, Mrs. Acuña-Rodriguez, it was Annie! That bad accident—it was Annie!"

Twenty-year-old Annie Rodriguez drove out of the grocery store parking lot, approached the intersection, then shifted into gear as the light turned green. Another driver approaching the intersection ran the opposing red and T-boned Annie at full speed.

The police reported that twenty people immediately stopped and attempted to care for Annie while 9-1-1 was called. Six of them remained on the scene until she was extracted by the Jaws of Life and airlifted several hours later.

The other driver walked away.

Annie screamed, then passed out. Her body had gone through the windshield, then back into the car. The seatbelt across her chest had snapped. The left side of her face was ripped open from the top of her forehead to under her chin. Her left index finger hung by a shred of skin. Her lips dangled open. Once the rescue squad got her out of the car, the coroner declared her dead due to blood loss.

But one of the paramedics would not give up. He ripped open her shirt to do CPR.

Annie came to, on the ground, in pain, with an unknown man on top of her. She screamed, "I'm going to sue you for rape!"

He ignored her and continued his work. She passed out again.

That Friday evening, two weeks before Christmas, not many doctors were on duty at Jackson Memorial Hospital. But a talented orthopedic surgeon was. And it was a good thing: all of Annie's ribs were broken; her clavicles were broken; her jaw was dislocated; her right arm was shattered from the wrist up; her ulna and radius punctured the skin; and her humerus was fractured.

She had no internal injuries.

The priest arrived. Annie's father refused to allow him to administer the last rites, so the priest, a stern man with a severe countenance, offered only prayers of blessing.

Days later, after the initial swelling had gone down, the doctor realized both of Annie's ankles were broken.

Annie went through multiple surgeries and intense pain. She had her arm suspended in the air in a special sling. Her jaw was wired shut. Her face was covered by a bandage. The doctors used skin from under her chin to help suture her face so the scars wouldn't be quite so obvious. She lost six weeks of memory.

After the surgeries were done and Annie was released from his care, the orthopedic surgeon continued to visit her regularly.

So did the paramedic.

And so did the priest, who continued to offer somber blessings.

Annie's parents and two sisters spent a lot of time at the hospital. But her cousins-many-times-removed were concerned that she didn't have anyone staying with her at night. When visiting hours were over, they began to hide: one under the bed and one in the bathroom.

The nurses didn't check too closely.

For Christmas, Annie's large Cuban family usually shared a feast. This year they snuck pureed Cuban food into the hospital so Annie, jaw still wired shut, could suck it through a straw. Her family stayed and ate with her.

Annie's boyfriend left her. At age twenty, he couldn't handle the idea of being with someone who might be permanently disfigured.

A nurse taught Annie to go in her mind to her happy place—the beach. She visited there a lot.

Annie's father decided Annie needed a real, live happy place. He redecorated a ground-floor room at her grandparents' home by the ocean. Annie would be able to see the beach without having to step into the harsh sun that could damage the delicate, healing skin on her face.

As her father drove her to the beach house, one of her first car trips since the accident, Annie became frightened, then hysterical. The trauma was rearing its ugly head, and it wouldn't stop.

Annie's father, fed up, finally said, "Well, do you want me to just put you in the trunk?"

Annie stared at him for a minute, then started to laugh.

After days of gazing out at the beach, Annie was becoming wistful. When would she get to visit the beach properly?

Her friends responded by organizing a beach party. A gaggle of twenty-somethings in swimsuits showed up one night when the moon was full. It was party time.

While Annie's rehabilitation was well under way, her arm was still propped up sideways from her body, stabilized to heal. One of her girlfriends was shocked to realize no one had shaved Annie's armpits since the car crash, so she got Annie all smoothed down again.

Now it was party time.

Annie spent months in physical therapy, occupational therapy, speech therapy. Some days she felt therapy'd out. Her family drove her to appointments. Her fellow church members drove her to appointments. Her friends drove her to appointments. Her neighbors drove her to appointments.

The ever-solemn priest continued to offer blessings. Her church family offered prayers and repeatedly called the local radio station asking for the community's prayers long after the accident.

So many people showed up for so long—all to help Annie return to normal life.

Eight months after the crash, Annie, leaning on her mother's arm, rejoined her church family at Sunday service.

The priest's face crumpled when he saw her. He started crying. "Now *you* are the blessing."

COMMUNITY SUMMARY

Community at its core is a unified body of individuals. It may be based on geography or interest. It may be family, friends, or neighbors. However defined, community possesses the practical and emotional support to help us move through a crisis toward stability.

While we depend on our community in crisis, we may have to politely manage or coordinate it to avoid overwhelm and use it most effectively. It's OK to vary our community and to keep parts of our community at arm's length when in crisis. If we find ourselves avoiding members of the community or trying to "protect" them, it may be wise to talk with a "safe stranger." A safe stranger is a trusted confidant during a period of crisis, who then typically exits our life so we can conclude one chapter and move on to the next.

Sometimes our community can fail us in crisis, whether due to fatigue, lack of size and skills, or oversight. Then we must decide if we have the fortitude to let the failure go, if we lovingly release that part of our community, or if we set aside the failure temporarily and look at it again later.

Even with the possibility of uplifting support or crushing disappointment, a community still offers the greatest potential for stabilizing us when we hit one of life's potholes. A community can provide the resources, the person-power, and the encouragement to pump up that third tire of our Vehicle of Life. In return, we can show them how to keep on driving, even when the road is bumpy.

Connection:
Finding Greater Meaning

At the heart of resilience is a belief in oneself—also a belief in something larger than oneself. Resilient people do not let adversity define them. —Hara Esteroff Marano, editor, *Psychology Today*

Beauford loved the sea. He walked barefoot up and down the shore every morning, occasionally nodding at people he passed or picking up seashells for his granddaughter, but more often simply looking to the distance. On weekends, he could go to the beach and do nothing but sit and watch the waves for hours.

With age and arthritis, Beauford reached the point he could no longer walk. He missed the ocean. He missed the sound of the waves breaking and the salt spray on his face. Beauford found himself melancholy more and more often.

When Terry, a nursing home volunteer, offered to take him to the beach, Beauford was ecstatic. He knew a visit to the ocean would fill his heart to brimming—the way it always had.

It was a hot July day, and Beauford had put on his favorite beachcomber shorts and sandals for the occasion. When they arrived at the strand, Terry, a tall, burly man, pushed Beauford in his wheelchair out to the very end of the boardwalk high over the crashing waves, where he could see all around. Beauford closed his eyes as he felt the sun on his face. He squinted into the breeze of the sea, watching the gulls fly over and hearing their squawks.

He looked up at Terry, puzzled. "There's something missing," he said. "There's just something missing." He shook his head.

Terry tried to help Beauford think of what might be missing, but no luck. They enjoyed the sea for a while longer. Finally Beauford shrugged his shoulders and said, "I guess it's time to go home."

As Terry pushed Beauford's wheelchair back off the boardwalk down the ramp, they hit a spot where the wheelchair jiggled, causing sand to come up over Beauford's feet. In that instant, his face flushed.

"Stop!" he cried. "Stop, stop, stop! That's what I need!"

Terry was completely perplexed, but stopped the wheelchair.

Beauford said, "You're a bigger guy than I am. Can you just hold me up for a minute and let me get my feet in the sand?"

Terry did.

The instant Beauford had his feet in that warm sand, he knew he'd found what he was looking for. He'd recovered that connection to the ocean, to himself, and to something bigger.

WHAT DO WE MEAN BY *CONNECTION*?

When we say *connection*, we're talking about connecting to something greater than ourselves. Dictionary definitions for *connection* are somewhat unsatisfying. The closest options from Merriam-Webster might be:

1. Contextual relation or association (Yes, we are trying to set our own life in context of something greater),
2. A relation of personal intimacy (Yes, by connecting to something or someone, we gain intimacy and self-understanding), or

3. Coherence, continuity (Yes, and maybe the most relevant, we are searching for coherence—we seek to understand how the diverse elements of life integrate; and we are searching in some ways for continuity—we want life to continue, and we want to know that we are part of that continuance).

In a nutshell, we want to put our lives in context so we understand our own role and importance in the universe and know that we are contributing to an ongoing good.

The Value of Connection

This C, Connection, is more ambiguous than the other three Cs. Language does not always capture the subtleties of Connection. Connection is that thing that touches our spirit. It is that thing that comforts, uplifts, sustains, and enriches us. Connection supercharges us like plugging a cord into an outlet.

All of these things that we are trying to describe make us feel connected to the world around us. They help fuel our sense of purpose, our sense of rootedness, our sense of groundedness. And when life has been disrupted by crisis or shock, to feel a connection that goes beyond self is indeed empowering.

We want to put our lives in context so we understand our role in the universe and know we are contributing to an ongoing good.

Unfortunately, we often say "If I have the time [or energy or capacity], I will..." and you can fill in the blank. "I will go to church." "I will join a choir." "I will go to a political rally." "I will take a walk in the woods." Frequently, the things that bring us joy and connection land on life's list of "extras."

How ironic. These "extras" stabilize us in a time of crisis. Because they reach to our core *stuff*, even a taste of them can make a big difference.

I use the word "stuff" with a lot of appreciation for what it means. Think of a child's soft toy. That teddy bear or velveteen rabbit is filled with stuffing; that's what makes it soft and snuggly. "Stuff" is what's inside of us that makes us more than just machines, more than just robots doing our jobs day in and day out. "Stuff" is the essence of our humanity. "Stuff" is where connection to something greater takes place.

There is an old expression: "He got the stuffing knocked out of him." When we go through a shock, there's a sort of blow to the solar plexus that takes our breath away and makes a dent in part of our being. If you have a serious traffic accident, in addition to your injuries, you're dealing with insurance companies, whose fault it is, whether the cars can be repaired or not, arranging alternate transportation, and the impact on your finances, AND you've got your regular job to perform. How likely is it, particularly in those first forty-eight to seventy-two hours, that you are going to say "I think I need to take a thirty-minute walk in the woods to reconnect with nature"? Not likely.

Yet for so many people, that connection, like a little slice of sunshine peeking through the clouds, is sometimes the most nourishing and enriching thing that could happen. But when people's lives are clouded by crisis, they may not realize that sunshine is there waiting for them.

Types of Connection

Many people, when they hear the phrase "connection to something greater than self," automatically think of religion or a deity (God, Buddha, Allah, etc.) and then connection to people who share that same belief or philosophy. That is indeed an important type of connection, which we'll explore shortly. While that form of connection is meaningful for many people, it is not meaningful for everyone. For a long time, I think, a broad group of folks felt left out because they didn't share religious feelings. Yet even without religion, there is still somehow an innate sense that *I am more than just me.*

I think we are beginning to create a more complete vocabulary around what it means to be connected to something greater, whether we can see, hear, touch, taste, or feel those aspects of life, and whether they are invisible around us or intrinsic within us. Consider these forms of connection:

- ❖ Philanthropy
- ❖ Music
- ❖ Arts and literature
- ❖ Sports
- ❖ Nature
- ❖ Heritage
- ❖ Social or political causes
- ❖ Shared challenges or experiences
- ❖ Professions
- ❖ Humor

We'll look at these in more depth later in this chapter.

Connection Is Personal

Each of us has our own form of connection. For some it's religion. For others it may be one of the things mentioned above. For Beauford it was a visceral connection to nature when he felt the warm sand on his feet.

You may know exactly what helps you feel connected and supercharged. Or you may not be so clear about what revs you up. Plenty of us, especially outside of crisis, just live our lives. We get up, we take care of the kids, we go to work, we garden, but we don't really pause to consider what defines our capital-C "Connection." And if we don't happen to be part of a religious group or some other obvious connection point, we might not be tuned in to this concept at all.

---

5 Ways to Connect When You Have Only 5 Minutes

1. Reconnect with someone from a happy time in your life. Look up an old friend on Facebook and send a quick message.
2. Play music you like as loudly as possible. Feel the music in your bones as well as hear it in your ears.
3. Get outside and take a walk. Stop and observe one thing of beauty. Really stare at it. Notice the colors, shapes, textures, fragrances, or sounds that remind you of the wonder of nature.
4. Send an email or text to someone in your favorite club or organization and ask for an update on the group's activities. Let the group know you look forward to participating as soon as you can.
5. Write a check or make an online donation to your favorite charity. Contributing to a cause that's meaningful to you ties you to that cause and enhances your self-esteem.

But I've observed that just because a primary connection hasn't been verbalized or put into an identified practice, most individuals still have something that connects them to an idea greater than self. It might be like a country song: "My mama's belief in me and all she thought I could be." Sometimes our meaning lives so deep down, we don't identify it—it's just part of us.

When people with no obvious connection hit crisis, do they suddenly develop a need for religion or connection to a greater good? The answer is definite: some do, and some don't.

QUESTIONS FOR REFLECTION

What makes me feel connected or supercharged?

How often do I focus or participate in this part of life?

How can I incorporate more of this element of connection into my life?

If I have only five minutes a day, what are some specific things I can do to feel that connection?

FINDING CONNECTION THROUGH
RELIGION AND SPIRITUALITY

Because religion and spirituality are such important methods of connection for so many people, I want to spend some time on them here. If you don't consider yourself religious or spiritual, you may want to skip ahead, and that's OK. If you choose to read this section, you may find some overarching principles that apply beyond religion and spirituality or that help you understand how others experience connection in a time of crisis.

Religion and Spirituality in the United States

Here in the United States we have a pluralistic society, with many different religions actively practiced. According to Pew Research Center (2014 data), about three-quarters (76.5%) of Americans claim an affiliation with some organized faith. A little under half of Americans (46.5%) are affiliated with Protestant churches, and around one-fifth (20.8%) are affiliated with Catholic churches. About six percent (5.9%) of Americans are affiliated with non-Christian faiths (Jewish, Buddhist, Muslim, Hindu, and others).

More than one-fifth (22.8%) of Americans describe themselves as religiously unaffiliated, and this number continues to grow. Just over seven percent (7.1%) describe themselves as atheist or agnostic, while nearly sixteen percent (15.8%) describe themselves as "nothing in particular." According to Pew's 2012 data, many of these "nones" say they believe in God (68%, with varying degrees of certainty), feel a deep connection with nature and the earth (58%), or classify themselves as "spiritual" but not "religious" (37%).

Across the spectrum of religion and spirituality, we see great variation in practice. Some people find a depth of meaning in strict adherence to their faith, while others find satisfaction in a looser interpretation. Still others combine aspects of various religions, whether based on where they've lived, people to whom they've been married, or their own spiritual preferences. For these people, religion is not an "either/or" proposition, but rather a "both/and."

Rituals in Religion and Spirituality

Guido immigrated to the United States from Italy as a young adult and maintained strong ties to his roots — the food, the culture, the Catholic faith. During the months he was receiving hospice care, my visits were primarily with his family. Guido occasionally felt strong enough to see me, but only for very short periods of time. The family appreciated and respected my presence, though as a female Protestant chaplain, I wasn't exactly what they were used to.

One Monday evening I got a crisis call. Guido's daughter felt that he might be in his final day; they couldn't reach their priest, so could I please come quickly? I hastily put on a black suit and a clerical shirt with the recognizable white tab collar, and rushed to the patient's home.

I said to the distressed family, "I realize you can't reach Father John right now, but would you like for us to gather around Guido's bed and say the Rosary?"

They were pleasantly surprised that a Protestant chaplain knew about the Rosary. I assured them that, having grown up outside Pittsburgh in a predominantly Roman Catholic community, I'd gone to Mass with my friends for many years and was quite comfortable with the prayers of their church.

Surrounding their beloved father, we made the sign of the cross, lifted ancient prayers, and gently caressed rosary beads worn smooth by decades of faithful worship. After the final amen, Guido's son dropped his hiked shoulders and voiced a gentle "Thank you," affirmed by silent nods from his brother and sister. Unfortunately, Guido's clenched jaw and furrowed brow told me he did not experience the same sense of peace.

Suddenly I remembered that I had Father John's private mobile number, reserved for only crisis calls. I snuck off to another room and reached him immediately.

"Becky," he said, "I'll be glad to come, but this is my day off and I'm in very casual clothes. I'm at Kinko's right now because the church's copy machine broke down." He paused. "I can come to the house, but I'm not going to look much like a priest."

I said, "I think Mr. Salvatore needs you to come, regardless of what you're wearing."

About fifteen minutes later, Father John rang the doorbell. Wearing jeans and a polo shirt, draped with his vestment stole, he carried the box containing the Eucharist. (Ministers learn early on to keep religious necessities in the car.) He invited me to join the family at Guido's bedside for the anointing of the sick (part of the last rites).

So, here stood the female Protestant chaplain in her black clerical clothes, and there stood the male Catholic priest in his red polo shirt, jeans, and clerical stole. Poor Guido must have been so confused he just couldn't die that night—he lived another two weeks!

Sometimes in the midst of crisis, our spirit just doesn't want us to be creative. It wants a very traditional, familiar way of doing things.

Examples of Religious and Spiritual Rituals

- **Prayer** – Typically a request for help, an offering of thanks, or giving of praise to a deity.
- **Meditation** – A way of quieting the mind and spirit, typically by sitting still and focusing on the breath or repeating a word or mantra.
- **Ceremony** – Typically a formal religious occasion (such as baptism, bar mitzvah, wedding, funeral), usually following particular protocols.
- **Liturgy** – The prescribed form of a worship service. This term is often used in Christianity, but other faith practices often follow an ordered form of worship, whether they use the term liturgy or not.
- **Sacrifice** – In previous times this might have been a blood sacrifice (e.g., the fatted calf). Modern examples include Christians who give something up for Lent and Muslims who fast during Ramadan. Sacrifice serves as a channel to come closer to God or Allah.
- **Pilgrimage** – A journey to a physical location associated with one's faith. Muslims travel to Mecca. Jews travel to the Wailing Wall in Jerusalem. Christians travel to the Holy Land.

Religion During Crisis

For those of us who follow a religion, whether closely or more loosely, several things can happen in a time of crisis:

❖ We may be **strengthened** and pulled more closely into the center of our religion.

❖ Our religious practice can be **disrupted**, which may cause additional anxiety.

❖ We may **lose** our connection to religion and find ourselves saying, "I don't believe this after all. This is not how I identify myself. This is not my connection."

❖ We may be **drawn back** to our religious roots.

Strengthening Our Connection

Some people very clearly have their primary connection via religion. In non-crisis times, they may sense a presence around them or within them. Some people see visions or have auditory experiences. In a time of crisis, maintaining this connection provides life-giving stability.

Those who have been more loosely connected to their faith may suddenly find it growing in importance. They may begin to attend church or temple more regularly. They may begin to call on the people in their faith community for assistance and emotional support.

Saul and Naomi contributed generously to their synagogue and always attended services on the High Holy Days. Saul even offered a discount to fellow synagogue members at his jewelry store. But regular attendance at worship? Not so much. Saul and Naomi invested every possible minute into their small but thriving business.

Then the recession hit. The town's economic anchor, a division of a large computer manufacturer, downsized its leadership team and outsourced much of its production. Not only did Saul and Naomi's customers lose their disposable income, many of them lost their homes and savings.

The community crisis brought Saul and Naomi to their own crisis—the threat of bankruptcy. Frightened, embarrassed, and uncertain of their future, they turned to their faith. Tearfully they told their rabbi that they could not maintain their current level of giving. Rabbi Schaumburg suggested that there were other ways they could not only give to the congregation, but could receive from the wisdom and bounty of their faith.

In Friday night worship Saul and Naomi rediscovered the beauty and spiritual nurture of the ancient scriptures. Reading from the Torah, listening to the cantor, and sensing the spirit of the congregation at worship filled this beleaguered couple with strength and renewed hope.

Not only did they attend services each week, but they used their professional skills to maintain the ornate relics donated to the synagogue.

Their newly energized faith did not cause a boom in the jewelry business, but it did help them calm down so they could make clearer decisions. They also met an attorney in the congregation who guided them through restructuring their business.

Now, five years after their crisis, Saul and Naomi remain faithful worship attendees.

Sometimes people in crisis not only strengthen their connection with their faith, but they take their faith to an extreme. You might see behavior such as:

- ❖ Sending large amounts of money to religious leaders on TV or radio for promises of cures, jobs, or a financial windfall
- ❖ Neglecting family, job, or other responsibilities to participate in religious services or events
- ❖ Unwillingness to act on practical advice or medical treatments due to belief that God will take care of everything without any human intervention

If you observe this behavior in a friend or family member, ask her about the changes she is making. It is important to hear if she is aware of the changes and what she thinks about them. Then, if you are part of her inner circle or have built a base of trust, ask her how this has affected her budget and time. Ask about the implications of not following professional advice.

Depending on the answer, you have a choice. Can you—without judgment—accompany that person and allow her choices to play out however they will? Or, is it your role to gently confront her or express your opinions, realizing that while it may create an "aha" for her, it may also create a disconnection between the two of you?

While this type of extreme behavior tends to manifest with religion, recognize it can happen in other arenas as well. Seek first to understand; understand how this behavior fits with your values and whether you can tolerate it. Then decide what degree of open discussion to pursue.

Being Disrupted in Our Practices

When religion is a strong connection point for someone, it can be unsettling when religious observances are disrupted. What happens when the faith practices that soothed your spirit are not available?

> *It can be unsettling when faith practices are interrupted.*

Take for instance a Muslim man whose practice is to kneel facing Mecca to pray at the prescribed hours of the day. What happens when he breaks his leg in a car accident and is physically unable to be on his knees? What if the accident was so bad he is confined to a hospital bed, disoriented from drugs and unaware of the time? He experiences a disruption in a religious practice that may be central to his core being.

For many Catholics, like Guido, going to Mass, making confession to a priest, and receiving the Eucharist are absolutely life-giving. When those things cannot take place in the normal manner, it can cause distress for a person in that faith practice.

Some people view their inability to participate in traditional forms of faith practice as a temporary disruption. Others find it wracks them with guilt, even when circumstances are out of their control. Still others find this "failure" to be an additional shock on top of the primary crisis.

When this sort of disruption occurs, try the following:

❖ Look for elements of meaningful practice that *can* be incorporated into the current situation. For example, if you cannot attend services, perhaps a religious leader or members of the church, synagogue, or temple could visit.

❖ Watch services on TV or video, read meditations, or listen to music from your faith.

❖ Seek counsel from your religious leader about how to remain observant. Within most religions, there are accommodations for those with some sort of limitation. In my experience, most people in need of accommodation feel more true to their faith practice when they've gained instruction and affirmation from that person in authority.

Losing Our Connection

Sometimes in crisis we find, temporarily or permanently, that our religious or spiritual connection has broken, changed, or lost meaning. This can be true particularly when our religion contains a dogma we no longer believe or we feel has, in the worst case, betrayed us.

My professional training is in the Christian faith, where there is a strong belief that God cares for us like a parent cares for a child. Sometimes that's interpreted as "If I am an obedient child, everything will be OK." When things are not OK, some people feel abandoned, which chops away at the root of their faith. Like a plant that can't get enough water, their faith withers and dies.

> *When possible, avoid making permanent decisions in the midst of crisis.*

I suggest that people in the midst of or freshly past a crisis refrain from making permanent decisions about faith. Sometimes it helps to identify the issue, set it aside temporarily, then reconsider it when the crisis has passed.

If you find yourself disconnecting from your religion, consider the following questions to help you sort through what is happening.

QUESTIONS FOR REFLECTION

Did my belief change due to the crisis, or has this been a gradual shift even before the crisis?

Do I want to return to my previous religious/spiritual connection?

Do I believe that this faith practice is not true, or do I simply not feel the same way about it right now?

Is there another type of connection that supports me better right now?

Do I want to make permanent changes or temporary adjustments to my religious connection?

Returning to Religious Roots

When I met Peter, he quickly told me that he and his wife were active members of the nearby Presbyterian church, so we based our hospice visits around that faith.

As Peter got weaker, I sensed he had some spiritual challenges that we just weren't resolving. His own minister visited on a regular basis as well, and still Peter wasn't finding peace. On a hunch, I asked Peter about his childhood. He told me he'd come from a blue-collar family in New Jersey.

I asked if by any chance he grew up going to the Roman Catholic church.

He sheepishly said, "Well, yeah, I was baptized and confirmed Catholic. I went to parochial school until seventh grade and was an altar boy. During my college years I went to the Presbyterian church with my friends, and never went back to the Catholic church."

I nodded. "I've noticed that when we're in stressful times, it helps reconnect to important parts of our childhood." I paused. "Do you think you'd like to see a priest?"

At first, Peter adamantly opposed the idea. Then, he made one excuse after the other why it was a bad idea. Finally, he said, "I'm afraid it would be disloyal to Pastor Williams and to my church now."

Ah. I assured him that wasn't the case. After some negotiation, he agreed to see a priest as long as Pastor Williams didn't know. I arranged for Father Miguel to visit, hear Peter's confession, and bring Holy Communion from the cathedral. After his visit Father Miguel smiled and told me, "I think this was important for Peter."

In times of trouble, value the significance of religious roots.

Over the next two months, Peter was able to reconcile both parts of his faith history within himself. Then, with his permission, we talked to Pastor Williams, who was relieved that Peter was getting the spiritual support he needed.

Peter's funeral was conducted in his Presbyterian church. Pastor Williams was the primary officiant, with Father Miguel and me assisting.

The adage "Make new friends, but keep the old. One is silver and the other gold" also applies to faith practices throughout life. Particularly in times of trouble, value the significance of religious roots.

FINDING CONNECTION OUTSIDE RELIGION AND SPIRITUALITY

Not everyone finds connection through religion or spirituality. Even those who are religious may find connection in a variety of places. Consider some of these forms of connection:

Philanthropy – For some people giving their time, money, and talents to a philanthropic organization gives their life meaning. Perhaps it's the Lions Club, which serves children with visual challenges. Perhaps it's the Junior League, a women's civic and volunteer service organization.

Music – Many people find that music says something words cannot, whether joyful, mournful, or somewhere in between.

Arts and literature – Human expression takes many forms, from painting to sculpture to poetry to ghost stories to ballet to hip-hop.

Sports – Both team and individual sports can challenge us to perform our best and fulfill our potential, from achieving a marathon PR (personal record) to learning to putt to watching a granddaughter play in the basketball state championship. Whether participating or observing, sports help us appreciate the human body's capabilities.

Nature – Some people love the beach, some people love the mountains, some are awed by the Great Plains of the Midwest. Sunrise and sunset, the sound of a thunderstorm, and the gentle lapping of the waves on the lakeshore—they all can touch us.

Heritage – Have you ever stopped to consider what life was like for your great-great-great-great-grandparents? Do you carry on traditions from "the old country"? Associations with the past, our family, and our culture provide a powerful foundation for connection.

Social or political causes – Groups who gather and share information, rally, petition, or lobby for a particular cause often experience a strong connection to both the cause and to each other. Political parties, social issues, and community causes create ethical and emotional bonds rooted in working for the greater good.

Shared challenges or experiences – When people have physical or mental challenges, disabilities, or illnesses, they often connect for support, education, or fundraising focused on improving that problem. Organizations like Alcoholics Anonymous and illness- or disability-related nonprofits and support groups may primarily function as resources for specific problems, but may also provide avenues for action, personal connection, and connection to a greater purpose.

Professions – Many people identify strongly with their profession. They often are part of an association that sets ethical and

> *Your significant connection may not appear on this list— stay open to possibilities!*

professional standards, provides continuing education on topics of interest and importance to that profession, and offers ways to contribute back to the profession. Whether the field is medicine, marketing, or music, the connection is to "the work" and the people doing it.

Humor – You might think humor is a funny item to have on this list (pun intended). Have you ever laughed at an odd joke and caught the eye of a stranger who also laughed? Did you feel that instant connection of a shared understanding? Humor is one of those oh-so-defining-but-hard-to-describe characteristics of being human and connecting with other humans.

Any one of the items on the list above can keep our Connection tire inflated on the Vehicle of Life. You may also find connection through something *not* on this list, so stay open to possibilities.

EXPANDING OUR CONNECTIONS

We humans have so many glorious parts and pieces about us. Sometimes we put our blinders on and think, "This one thing is my focus. This one thing gives me purpose. This one thing, when I'm feeling small, it's big, and I can be part of this one great big thing."

There's nothing wrong with having a primary point of connection, but if you lose that underpinning, it becomes tricky to keep your balance.

In crisis (and in the absence of crisis), I encourage people to expand their points of connection. As powerful as it is to call on one primary connection, it empowers us even further to have other sources of strength to draw from.

For example, Zelda's Jewish faith brings great meaning to her life, but for her, connection goes beyond the Torah, the synagogue, and her son's bar mitzvah. She also feels strongly connected to the arts. When she's in stressful times, she revels in walking through art galleries. She recently decided to take a pottery class to feel a physical as well as emotional connection. She also gains strength from donating to arts groups, and when she's particularly low, she makes a point to write a note to an artist, "I just saw your work, and it lifted my soul."

> *One primary connection increases stability. Additional connections offer reinforcement.*

Use the following reflection questions to explore ways to expand your connections. Find your own personal mix of things that help you feel connected to something beyond self.

QUESTIONS FOR REFLECTION

What experiences, beliefs, or activities generate a sense of:

Excitement	*Trust*
Calm	*Energy*
Increased self-esteem	*Anticipation*
Patriotism	*Accomplishment*
Fun	*Hope*
Groundedness	

Consider the possible connections listed earlier. What feelings do those suggestions generate in you?

Which ideas bring a positive physical and emotional reaction?

Which ideas seem like something you want to explore?

ENCOURAGING CONNECTION

Your elderly neighbor, with whom you've had heated political debates, has suffered a fall and is now in a rehab facility two hours away, close to his family. The election is only a few days off. Your neighbor ordered an absentee ballot, but when you go to check his mail, you realize they sent it to his home address rather than the rehab's address. You're afraid the post office won't get it there in time, so you drive two hours to take him his mail, including the absentee ballot.

What a powerful way to reconnect your neighbor to what's important to him and to help him regain some semblance of normal life.

When we walk alongside people in crisis, it can feel difficult to know what to offer them. To encourage connection for others, I have two pieces of guidance:

- ❖ Don't impose your own form of connection
- ❖ Dig beneath the surface to find the right connection

Don't Impose Your Own Connection

We sometimes assume everyone shares the same beliefs or values we do. They may or may not. Remember the Platinum Rule: Do unto others *as they want to be done unto.*

In particular, when it comes to connection, we must be cautious about imposing our own religious or spiritual beliefs on someone who doesn't share them.

If you impose your beliefs on someone else, you can cause:

- ❖ **Shut-down** – The other person may stop talking, withdraw, or edit her comments before she speaks.
- ❖ **Defensiveness** – The other person may start defending or justifying her own beliefs.
- ❖ **Guilt** – The other person may feel she *should* feel the way you do—even if she doesn't. Rather than inspiring or opening up possibilities, you just make her feel bad.
- ❖ **Alienation** – The other person may feel so alienated that she disconnects from you completely.

But this guideline applies to any other form of connection as well, not just religion. Not everyone gets thrills from nature or from choral music. Not everyone sits on the same side of the political aisle.

As shock absorbers for those in crisis, part of what we can do is listen closely to spoken and unspoken messages about what brings other people a sense of connection.

CAUTION: Don't impose your own religious or spiritual beliefs on someone who doesn't share them.

The same suggestions that we discussed in the Comfort chapter apply here:

❖ Pay attention
❖ Listen carefully
❖ Ask questions
❖ Gain permission to speak

Rather than racing as quickly as possible to what you think the destination is, try exploring the topic with the person you are walking alongside. Don't be afraid to take some side paths; they may lead you in unexpected directions.

For example, you might say, "I can see this is a tough time. Are there things that are giving you hope right now?" When the person in crisis responds, do you hear in his words or see in his body language anything that would give you clues as to what may be meaningful to him? Does he use religious language? Non-religious language? Does he describe other sorts of connections?

Follow the path he heads down from a position of curiosity, without being false or disingenuous about it. But don't stop at the surface.

Dig Deeper to Find the Right Connection

Your friend Rhonda has been going through a rough patch after losing her mother. She loves the theater, so you think it would be special to take her to a play. You purchase tickets to Shakespeare in the Park and pick her up for the Sunday afternoon performance. Afterward you find out Rhonda loves avant-garde theater, so Shakespeare didn't provide quite the response you'd hoped for. Rhonda felt supported, but she didn't have that feet-in-the-warm-sand experience.

Finding someone's meaningful forms of connection is like unwrapping a package with a knotted cord on top. The package might be a gorgeously wrapped box from a department store, or it might be a tattered old box hidden away in the garage for years. You can't get inside the package to see what's there until you carefully unknot that cord. Sure, you could hack it open with a knife, but you'd destroy something in the process. It's better to work at loosening that knot until you can remove the wrapping, open the package, and see what's inside.

When you accompany a person in crisis, you're untying the knots and very gently removing the covering so you can understand what is deepest inside that person. Only then can you honor and encourage it.

QUESTIONS FOR REFLECTION

Are there subjects that stir visible emotion in this person? Excitement? Calm? Joy? Enthusiasm?

What people, organizations, or events are key elements to this topic?

Does the person have an ongoing involvement with this topic, or is it something enjoyed just once or twice?

Is there any way for the person in crisis to participate now?

Can you assist that person in making a connection to something meaningful?

HIGHLIGHT STORY: A SPECIAL GLOW

I'll never forget visiting with my hospice patient Ned Johnson. We had a wonderful connection, and I knew that he valued my visits as a chaplain.

One day I said, "Ned, you've got a special glow about you today."

He grinned. "Yeah, I really do."

I asked what was going on.

"Oh, man," he said. "I had a great visit yesterday."

Well, *that* took me down a peg. I hadn't been to see Ned the day before, so I knew his great visit wasn't with me! I thought, *Okay, well, maybe the nurse or the social worker had been here.*

I asked (cheerfully), "Who was here yesterday, Ned?"

He said, "It was my volunteer."

I thought, *Wow, we've just knocked out the whole clinical staff. Now the volunteer is on top!*

I kept going. "Well, Ned, what did you talk about?"

He said, "Talk? We didn't talk about anything. We watched a football game!"

Frankly, knowing his volunteer as I did, Carlos probably didn't have a whole lot to talk about with Ned. A big-hearted guy, Carlos showed caring through action, not words. I don't know if he simply ran across a football game on TV or if he genuinely knew how much Ned loved football. Either way, it worked. And *that* was Ned's great visit. Watching a football game with another guy.

To this day I have a picture in my head of Ned and Carlos sitting in their recliners, nodding occasionally at each other after a good play. And in my mental image, Ned is thinking to himself *I may not be able to get out and mow the yard anymore or change the oil in the car, but I'm still a man and I'm watching football with another man.*

That's a powerful connection.

CONNECTION SUMMARY

Connection is that thing that touches our spirit. It is that thing that comforts, uplifts, sustains, and enriches us. In a nutshell, we want to put our lives in context so we understand our own role and importance in the universe and know that we are contributing to an ongoing good.

Connection is personal. We may find it in any number of ways: philanthropy, music, art, literature, sports, nature, heritage, religion, spirituality, humor. As with Comfort, Connection may come through rituals and traditions. In crisis, Connection brings us purpose, meaning, and strength to carry on in the face of difficulties.

Our connection to religion in particular can be affected by crisis. We may find ourselves strengthening our connection, having our religious practices disrupted, losing our connection, or returning to our religious roots after being away. Religious or not, any form of connection is subject to shifts due to a crisis.

Expanding our own connections in daily life and encouraging connection for others inflates that tire on our Vehicle of Life, better positioning us to move through crises when they hit. As with the other Cs, remember Connection is personal; ask questions and listen closely to find the right connection for the person in crisis.

Part 2:
The E-A-R Road to Resilience

Experience: Learning from the Past
Assumptions: Steering in the Right Direction
Resources: Taking Stock

Experience:
Learning from the Past

Those who cannot remember the past are condemned to repeat it.
—George Santayana

How could this have happened? Kyle and Amanda exchanged looks of bewilderment, then accusation, and finally horror before they stumbled out of their CPA's office.

Kyle's work as a computer programmer and Amanda's as a realtor provided a comfortable life for them and their two teenagers, but the past year had created challenges—challenges they thought they'd handled well. Now they weren't so sure.

When seventeen-year-old Logan totaled his car, they dipped into their savings account, grateful to have it for this emergency. But between uncovered medical bills, replacing his "starter car" with a safer one, and increased insurance premiums, their account quickly evaporated.

Logan's hospitalization lasted a week, but his rehab stretched out for months. At first Amanda juggled her clients around Logan's medical appointments, but when she double-booked herself multiple times and began making mistakes in her paperwork, she and her broker-in-charge agreed it would be best for Amanda to take family medical leave. Kyle and Amanda recognized they would have to manage on one income for a while and reasoned they could stay afloat by cutting back and using their emergency credit cards if things got too tight.

Logan took so much time and attention, they worried that thirteen-year-old Rain felt neglected. They enrolled her in a soccer camp she'd been begging to attend and rejoiced when she qualified for the elite team. Then they saw the fees for dues, equipment, and travel. Ouch. But one of the emergency credit cards and a modest withdrawal from their 401(k) would pay for everything.

Something new seemed to pop up every month: Amanda's car needed new brakes; the furnace had to be replaced; their dog needed multiple visits to the vet. They started paying only the minimum required amount on the credit cards each month. As soon as things got back to normal, they told themselves, they'd get everything paid off.

Then came the one-two punch. Monday they received a reminder notice of the sizeable withdrawal they had made from their 401(k) the previous year; since it hadn't been repaid, taxes and a penalty were now due. And Tuesday Kyle learned that his department was reorganizing. He could accept a lower-paying position or look for a new job.

With the credit card bills racking up interest, savings depleted, and a large tax bill staring them in the face, Kyle and Amanda weren't sure how they would pay the mortgage on Kyle's lower salary.

Their CPA suggested a route they had not allowed themselves to consider: bankruptcy.

WHAT DO WE MEAN BY *EXPERIENCE*?

Merriam-Webster offers several definitions for *experience*:

1. The process of doing and seeing things and of having things happen to you
2. Skill or knowledge that you get by doing something
3. The conscious events that make up an individual life

In the car metaphor we've been using throughout this book, experience is the frame of the car. It is the thing that contains us, protects us, and offers a window to look through.

The Value of Experience

Many of us grew up hearing the proverb "Experience is the best teacher," though perhaps we did not hear the Norwegian version, which adds the phrase "but the tuition is high."

Life is like a school with multiple ways to learn:

❖ As **students**, where we first read, study, and observe before doing something;

❖ As **apprentices**, where we work with someone more experienced, who gradually gives us opportunities to try things ourselves; or

❖ As **independent learners**, where we attempt something, and if it doesn't work out, we simply try another way.

Any of these approaches can give us the opportunity to use, evaluate, and retain or discard a particular approach. We can then use the lessons from that experience the next time we encounter a similar situation.

When we use our experience in a positive way:

❖ We have the opportunity to find information, which teaches us how to find more information; once found, we can choose to keep or discard the information.

❖ We have a realistic gauge of our talents and strengths.

❖ We have an understanding of our personal style of response.

❖ We boost our confidence and ability to cope with disruption.

Types of Crisis Experience

Awareness of your experience level with different types of crises may provide a clearer perspective of how sturdy your frame of experience is. Recall the types of crisis we discussed in the Overview chapter (see Figure 8):

❖ **Difficulty** – A relatively mild crisis, inconvenient but manageable.

❖ **Acute Crisis** – A crisis that happens suddenly and lasts a relatively short time. While there may be longer-term implications, the crisis situation itself is resolved.

❖ **Chronic Crisis** – A crisis that is of longer duration, or a series of recurring crises. Chronic crises may cause significant disruption or fairly little disruption.

❖ **Life-Altering Change** – A dramatic crisis that requires a complete realignment of how we live.

Figure 8 Types of Crisis

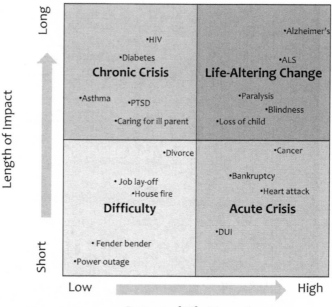

Remember, these categories are relative. *Your* experience, assumptions, and resources may shift where you place a particular crisis in this matrix.

By understanding the type of crisis you are in, you can better use prior experience to help move through it.

Memory and Therapy

What if I can't remember the past? What if I've had a terrible experience and prefer to forget it?

First, it's normal to forget some things. "Too much information can bog down the brain," says Sandra Bond Chapman, Ph.D., founder and chief director of the Center for BrainHealth at the University of Texas at Dallas. "If we had to remember every single thing we were ever exposed to, we probably couldn't do higher-order thinking or make decisions."

Second, hanging on to negative memories is not necessarily healthy. In fact the brain has a process that eliminates "unnecessary" memories. We can become directly involved in this process by exploring memories we think may be important, then decide whether we will hold on to them or "actively forget" them.

If you can't remember your own past, find someone with a similar past. You can still benefit from assessing experience, even if it is not your own. And as you learn from others, your own experience may come back. Sometimes childhood memories suddenly flash into focus.

But if you're concerned you've forgotten something important, crucial, or traumatic, you may need to talk with someone who can help you on an individual basis. This book cannot help you with repressed memories or psychological trauma. A mental health professional such as a therapist or psychologist may be appropriate.

A METHODICAL APPROACH TO USING EXPERIENCE TO DEAL WITH CRISIS

When we suffer a shock, we first need to stabilize (in particular by using the Four Cs), then we can start moving through the crisis, past our initial reaction and toward resilience. Having a simple, methodical process helps.

We begin by assessing our experience and asking a series of progressive questions:

1. Have I experienced **this situation** before? If so, what can I apply from that experience?

2. Have I experienced **anything like this** before? If so, what can I apply from that experience?

3. Has anyone in my **inner circle** or **outer circle** had this experience or one like it before? If so, what can they help me learn about it?

4. What else do I know that can help **mitigate the problem** even if I can't solve it?

Let's consider some examples that expand on these steps.

Assess Your Prior Experience with This Situation

When hit with a crisis ask yourself:

❖ Have I experienced **this situation** before?

❖ If so, what can I apply from that experience?

If you have experience with that same shock, you are more likely to regain control or ease the pain.

Example: Juanita was laid off from her job at the mortgage company. It was a shock at first, but then she realized this was the third time she'd been laid off. After her first layoff, she'd developed a habit of tracking her accomplishments at work so she could update her resume annually. She'd also started putting all her raises into a savings account. After her second layoff, she'd become more active in networking and maintaining relationships with people outside her own company. Both times before, she'd landed on her feet. She knew the economy was tougher now, but she was in about as good a shape as possible, all things considered. She knew what to do.

Example: Shantel got a 3 a.m. call from the answering service monitoring her eighty-four-year-old mother's medical alert button. She'd fallen in the bathroom, and EMS was on the way. As Shantel raced across town to the ER, she was thankful for the advice given by the hospital social worker after her mother had fallen the previous year. They'd added the med-alert button for emergency service and installed a lockbox with a house key so EMS could reach her mother if Shantel couldn't be there. They'd also printed a medication list to keep in her mother's bedside table as well as in the glove compartment of Shantel's car. Crisis didn't care about Shantel's convenience, so Shantel decided to be prepared.

Assess Your Prior Experience with Similar Situations

If you've not been through this exact crisis before, ask yourself:

- ❖ Have I experienced **anything like this** before?
- ❖ If so, what can I apply from that experience?

Even a parallel experience can bring to mind lessons, tools, and resources that pave the road to resilience.

Example: When George and Kevin's restaurant went up in flames due to a grease fire, they were distraught. But they quickly reflected on the time ten years prior that their garage had been wrecked by a tornado. They drew on that experience to clean up and assess the damage, to deal with the insurance company, and to find contractors for rebuilding. Kevin also used his experience as the restaurant's marketing manager to communicate with customers about their plans and to garner moral support. While it would be difficult to call the fire a blessing, George and Kevin were able to rebuild and enhance the restaurant within six months.

Example: In 1996 Hurricane Fran slammed Raleigh, creating major property damage and long-lasting power outages. I learned some lessons about resilience from the family of a hospice patient. An older couple, they lived way out in the country and had to wait longer than most for power to be restored. They revisited their growing-up years to find alternative ways of making life work.

They pulled waterproof boxes out of the storage shed, put the perishable food in them, and dropped them in a cold spring—instant refrigeration. They fired up the kerosene lanterns, which lasted much longer than flashlights. They woke up and went to sleep with the sun. They focused on contentment: being satisfied with what they had, making things last, or finding another way to make things work. And then, when nothing worked, they relaxed on the porch and played checkers.

Resilience indeed.

Learn from Others' Experience

We can take those first two steps, assessing our previous experience with the same or similar situations, on our own. But what happens when we haven't experienced anything like this crisis? We might need a hand to hold.

Ask yourself:

❖ Is there anyone in my **inner circle** or **outer circle** who has had this experience or one like it before?

❖ If so, what can they help me learn about it?

Find someone you trust who you feel comfortable calling on to ask, "What did you learn from this? Could you give me some insights?" This is another place where talking with a safe stranger can help.

Example: Wanda was diagnosed with breast cancer. Since about one in eight women gets breast cancer sometime in her life, Wanda, at age fifty-five, had several friends and relatives who had experienced it. She was able to call on them for advice and support during her treatment regimen.

Example: Ahmed returned from serving in the Army with a Purple Heart after being hit by an IED (improvised explosive device). He lost a leg as a result. Ahmed had never known anyone with an amputated limb or who used a prosthetic, at least not that he remembered. He found support through the Wounded Warrior project, which offered him not only resources to help with his physical change but also with the related emotional adjustments.

When Lacking in Experience, Leverage What You Have

A real challenge arises when we feel that neither we nor anyone in our community has experience that relates to our current crisis—or we don't have the time to find someone who does. Then ask:

❖ What else do I know that can help **mitigate the problem** even if I can't solve it?

❖ What is the **real challenge** in this particular experience that I'm going through right now?

❖ What do I see in this experience—even if it's new to me—that I can work with based on **my natural strengths**?

Example: I mentioned earlier that I am not a technical guru (to say the least). Let's say I'm working alone and have an important business proposal that has to be submitted using a particular technology. Let's also say I'm under a tight timeline and have a lot of revenue riding on this potential contract. I don't have experience with the technology. I don't have much experience solving technology problems generally. I don't have someone to consult on this technology.

This is where resilience comes in. Even though I am on shaky ground, I ask myself, "What do I know how to do that might help me in this crisis? The clock is ticking. What do I have to do to get this done?" My technology problem might not go away, but I may be able to work around it.

I start scrolling through my other experiences and thinking about ways to mitigate the problem.

❖ "I know I have the phone number and email for one person at the agency requesting the proposal. Maybe that person will have suggestions."

❖ "Maybe there's an alternate means of submission. Maybe I can email it or fax the document."

❖ "Maybe I can get an extension because of technology problems."

While getting the proposal submitted within acceptable guidelines is the ultimate objective, my personal challenge is avoiding panic about my technical skills. I look for anything I have that may offer even momentary stability. Stability allows panic and fear to subside so I can take the next step forward.

This allows me to recognize that I have a couple of strengths to leverage:

❖ I have a strong reputation for "following the rules" and submitting things on time, so there's a good chance my contact at the agency will allow some leeway.

❖ I am good on the phone. I can smoothly describe my problem, politely ask for assistance, and graciously thank whoever helps me.

As long as I can manage my technology-panic, things may turn out just fine.

Clearly my technology crisis fell into the "difficulty" quadrant of our crisis matrix. It was of short duration and low impact. But keep in mind the same process applies to more serious situations as well.

Kyle and Amanda, shocked at the thought of filing for bankruptcy, reluctantly visited Marlene Branch, the bankruptcy attorney their CPA recommended. Shame, anger, and fear engulfed them as they walked in the door, but Marlene's non-judgmental, informative approach calmed them.

After asking enough questions to understand the big picture, Marlene gave Kyle and Amanda a homework assignment. In addition to listing their assets and liabilities, she asked them to describe how they made financial decisions, both now and in the past. How did they manage things normally? What did they do when they had big bills or unexpected expenses?

Kyle and Amanda set aside time to reflect on the first years of their marriage. Even with a modest income and two young children, they had managed to pay their bills and save money each month. They pinpointed three key reasons:

1. They created a budget and then made a game out of keeping it.

2. They considered every purchase, even when the children asked, "Why can't I have that?"

3. Their friends were similarly frugal. If Kyle and Amanda didn't know where to find a bargain, one of their friends did.

When Kyle received a promotion that brought a significantly higher salary, they had purchased a bigger house in a new neighborhood and no longer felt the need for the budget game. Instead of one credit card paid off monthly, they now felt comfortable with rolling balances on three cards; plus, they had spare "emergency" cards. The kids rarely heard "no" to their requests for toys, games, or sports equipment. They lived like their new friends and neighbors did.

During Kyle and Amanda's second appointment with Marlene, she explained how filing for Chapter 13 bankruptcy would allow them to remain in their home, while repaying their debts over a three- to five-year period. Their debts wouldn't be eliminated, but Kyle and Amanda would have a workable plan for paying them down while keeping on top of current bills. Kyle and Amanda swallowed hard and kept listening.

"The thing is," Marlene said, "your monthly income has to be high enough for you to meet your mortgage and cover other costs and attorney's fees in order for your Chapter 13 bankruptcy plan to be considered feasible. If it's not, your plan wouldn't be confirmed. I think we'll need to wait until Amanda is back at work and making commissions again before filing. How long did you say you have left on your family medical leave, Amanda?"

"Four weeks," Amanda replied, "but won't waiting just get us in deeper? Can we really wait that long?"

Marlene nodded. "A little deeper, but if we start working on the plan now, we shouldn't have any problem getting it approved."

It was agreed: they would start planning to file for bankruptcy. Marlene referred them to a program where they could meet with a financial counselor to help them refresh their budgeting skills; there was even a peer group available, if they chose to participate.

Kyle and Amanda's wounded pride gave way to relief, and eventually confidence, as they benefitted from professional advice, peer support, and their own experience.

Now their whole family plays the budget game.

Sometimes it may feel like everything in your current crisis (or crises) needs to be addressed immediately. In reality there is often a window of time to take a breath before moving from one problem to the next. As Amanda and Kyle found, they could stop and focus on their son's health, then get Amanda back to work (more normalcy and control) before they had to tackle the bankruptcy process. While crisis-related drama can feel endless, watch for points where you can take a break.

> *Look for times when you can step away from crisis-related drama—even just briefly.*

Once you learn to look at your experience and leverage it in a crisis, you begin to develop a toolkit for future crises.

QUESTIONS FOR REFLECTION

What is the crisis I am dealing with currently?

*Have I experienced **this situation** before? If so, what can I apply from that experience?*

QUESTIONS FOR REFLECTION *continued*

*Have I experienced **anything like this** before? If so, what can I apply from that experience?*

*Has anyone in my **inner circle** or **outer circle** had this experience or one like it before? If so, what can they help me learn about it?*

*What else do I know that can help **mitigate the problem** even if I can't solve it?*

*What is the **real challenge** in this particular experience that I'm going through right now?*

*What do I see in this experience —even if it's new to me —that I can work with based on **my natural strengths**?*

OTHER TOOLS TO MANAGE YOUR EXPERIENCE

Earlier we talked about some of the things that happen when we are in crisis:

* ❖ **Physical** – Changes or extremes in physical patterns such as sleep and eating
* ❖ **Mental** – Difficulty concentrating, remembering things, and making decisions
* ❖ **Emotional** – Heightened sensitivity and responses, feeling overwhelmed, exaggerated communication patterns
* ❖ **Spiritual** – Changes or extremes in religious beliefs, searching for "why"

Tapping into the Four Cs of Stability (Comfort, Control, Community, and Connection) can help us regain our footing to move through the experience.

We may also benefit from some simple tools to help us manage the actual experience, in particular for some of the normal mental challenges we face in crisis, such as the inability to think clearly or remember things correctly. Some useful tools are:

* ❖ Gathering information
* ❖ Journaling
* ❖ Having someone else take notes
* ❖ Talking to a safe stranger

Gather Information

Some people stabilize during crisis when they obtain relevant information about their situation. Getting facts can help de-escalate the sense of fear that comes with crisis and increase the sense of control. Information may include expanded options, the experiences of others, or examples of ways to handle certain situations.

Information gathering is important and a good place to start managing your experience. One caution about information gathering: be aware of the extremes (see Figure 9).

Figure 9 Information-Gathering Continuum

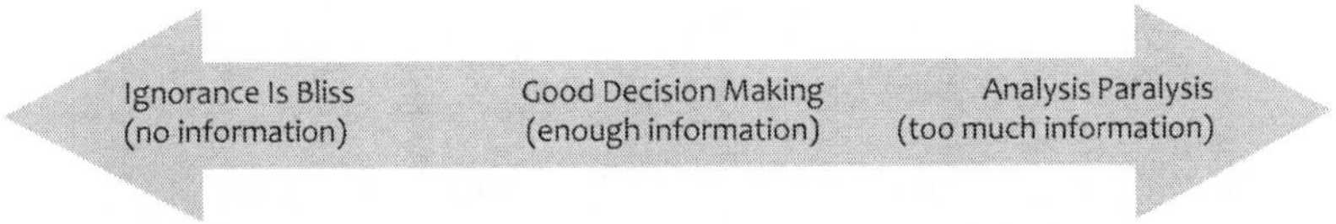

Ignorance Is Bliss (no information) — Good Decision Making (enough information) — Analysis Paralysis (too much information)

For example, Fatima is a recently displaced executive starting a job search. She hasn't had to apply for jobs in years. It's time to sharpen up her resume. Looking at the spectrum above, for Fatima:

* **Ignorance is bliss** equates to using the same resume she started with twenty years ago, only adding her professional experience without updating for format, style, or computerized search requirements.

* **Good decision-making** would be getting online to find a half dozen executive resumes targeted toward the type of position she's seeking, and using those as her starting point before taking her resume to an executive recruiter.

* **Analysis paralysis** could manifest as spending an excessive amount of time online looking at tens or hundreds of resume examples and constantly tweaking what she has, without actually taking steps to send her resume to anyone.

As with many things, finding the right balance with information gathering is key.

Keep a Journal

Some people write in a journal daily as a matter of course. They capture what happens in their day, process life's events, or just capture whatever comes to mind.

When in crisis, a new layer of value may come from journaling. You may find yourself writing about your feelings. As we've discussed, crisis can make you feel powerless or uncomfortable. Journaling can be your emotional "dumping ground," but it can also help you identify ways to get back to balance with your Four Cs, or to gain insights about why you feel the way you do.

You may find that you have trouble remembering things. Journaling helps capture important memories of the crisis you are going through, but also lets you write down practical to-do's, reminders, and critical pieces of information. "Met with Dr. Venzon today and discussed a possible procedure." Of course these things are going to be in your medical records, but you may be surprised at some of the related thoughts that surface. "Remembered how miserable Uncle Gerald was after that procedure, and I said I would never have it." Something flashes through your mind; unless you write it down, it might not come back.

Many people find the tactile sense of writing pen on paper to be most satisfying; there is a slower thoughtfulness that comes from moving your hand across the page. But whether you take notes on paper, on your computer, or on your smart phone, journaling can become a valuable source of comfort and practicality.

Have Someone Take Notes for You

When in crisis, people often find themselves in unfamiliar situations with a lot of information coming at them. Consider an illness where you see multiple doctors, or the death of a loved one where suddenly you are managing financial matters. These are times when it is helpful to have someone with you at appointments to take notes. Find someone you trust with your personal information, but also consider someone who is not too close to the immediate situation. Recall that distance from the crisis allows for more objectivity and clarity. Notes can be invaluable for a person in crisis to refer to later or to share with others who have a vested interest in the situation.

Find a Safe Stranger

We talked about safe strangers back in the Community chapter. Safe strangers can be more objective than we typically are when in crisis. They can ask questions and help us process our experience.

The simple act of speaking a fear out loud can lessen its magnitude. And even if the fear is a reality, speaking it aloud can open the space for you to be able to address it. Whether a subject-

> **SAFE STRANGERS**
>
> *People who come into our lives during crisis that we quickly bond with, but that also have a "distance" to them.*

matter expert, a therapist or counselor, or a close-but-not-too-close friend, a safe stranger can help manage anxiety and bring comfort and clarity in a difficult time.

QUESTIONS FOR REFLECTION

How am I managing my current crisis?

Is there something else I could add that would benefit me?

WALKING ALONGSIDE SOMEONE IN CRISIS

So far in this chapter we've talked about experience from the perspective of the person at the center of crisis. While it's helpful for members of the inner circle and outer circle to understand and share the process and tools we've discussed, there are some other pieces of experience that come into play as well.

As we walk alongside those in crisis, we can accompany them more effectively if we:

- ❖ Remember our own role,
- ❖ Avoid common pitfalls associated with that role, and
- ❖ Intentionally assess how we can best be of help.

One evening after a long day, I relaxed by reading the paper over dinner. A headline caught my eye. Someone had been killed in a car accident. Normally I skim the first paragraph of accident articles and move on. This time, as soon as I saw the names, I literally dropped my fork.

Back in the mid-1990s, I had a hospice patient, Melvin, with an adult daughter, Karen. I got to know Karen extremely well over the course of a year. After Mel died, Karen and I crossed paths frequently, so for several years I knew her moderately well. Shortly after her father died, Karen met Hal. A midlife marriage was a happy and unexpected surprise for them both. Then circumstances led Karen and me in different directions, and we got to the point where we bumped into each other about once a year. We have common acquaintances in the community, but no shared close friends.

Karen and Hal had been hit by a drunken driver. Hal was killed, and Karen was seriously injured.

I immediately thought, "I need to find out what hospital she's in and go comfort her."

As I sat alone in my kitchen with all these emotions and memories bubbling up, I texted someone who was close to me back when I saw Karen frequently.

He responded quickly, "I remember your friendship with Karen, and I'm so sorry for you as well as for her." Just to touch base with somebody who knew me during that timeframe stabilized me.

He continued, "You may want to find some way to process this, because it obviously touched a very deep spot in you."

He was right. I went for a walk. A slow, ponderous walk. By the time I came back, I had been able to sort through the pieces. I realized I played one role twenty years ago, and a different role now. I was part of Karen's inner circle then, but barely part of her outer circle now.

Your Role and Experience in Someone Else's Crisis

In this book, we've looked at three groups of people, based on their proximity to the crisis (Figure 10):

❖ **The individual in crisis** – The person who has experienced the main shock from the crisis.

❖ **Members of the "inner circle"** – Usually immediate family members and close friends.

❖ **Members of the "outer circle"** – Extended family members, friends, and the broader community, such as neighbors and colleagues.

As you walk alongside someone in crisis, keep in mind how your distance from the bull's-eye influences the ways in which you can best help that person.

Figure 10 Roles and Proximity to Crisis

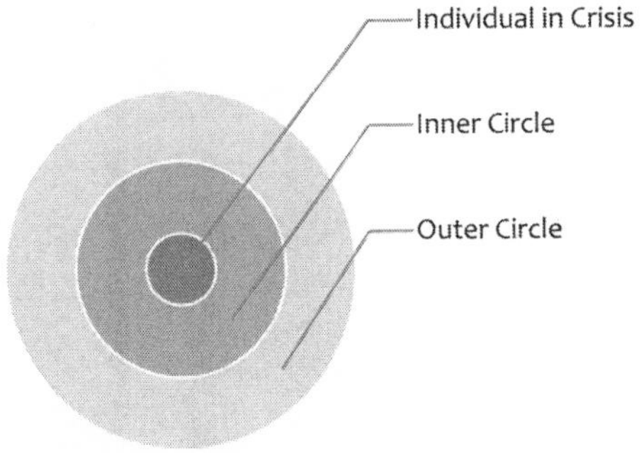

Individual in Crisis

Inner Circle

Outer Circle

Recall also, the common patterns of response to different types of crises (Figure 11). Understanding what you may see from the individual in crisis is helpful, but also note what you as a member of the inner or outer circle may experience. (I'll repeat myself: this is only a model. While these general patterns appear frequently, characteristics from any box may show up in your crisis situation.)

Figure 11 Common Responses to Different Types of Crisis by Role

	Individual in Crisis	Inner Circle	Outer Circle
Difficulty (Small fire)	• Feel surge of anxiety or clarity • Feel comfort and control affected • Feel the problem can be handled eventually	• Pull together • Do whatever it takes • Understand resources needed	• Offer help within limits • Require clear direction • Assess connection to the individual or situation to decide level of involvement
Acute Crisis (Temporary job loss)	• Experience panic, confusion, or bewilderment • Feel fear of death or permanent loss • Find unanticipated calm	• Either pull together or watch a solitary hero emerge • Do whatever it takes • Desire to be either hands-on doer or hands-off adviser	• Offer help within limits • Require clear direction • Assess connection to the individual or situation to decide level of involvement
Chronic Crisis (HIV diagnosis)	• Cope well, or complain • Become either a victim or a crusader regarding the problem • Pursue outward focus to avoid self-focus as well as to retain connection to others	• Feel sustainability of relationships and resources tested • Develop effective coping systems • Become silent or vocal martyr • Feel desire for interests outside the chronic problem • Experience shift in roles	• When called on, initially offer help willingly • Have occasional short-term involvement, but often get tired and fade away over time • Feel guilt or shame for not doing more • Don't realize an issue still exists
Life-Altering Change (Limb amputation)	• Experience post-traumatic stress or post-traumatic growth • Experience either depression or a heightened reason for being • Enter new communities • Increase search for meaning and connection beyond self	• Find relationships either torn apart or cemented • Develop effective coping strategies • Change priorities • Become involved with new communities • Experience shift in roles	• Become comfortable with changes and have normal relationship with individual in crisis • Feel too uncomfortable for direct involvement • Champion a cause on behalf of the individual • Discontinue all connection

Common Pitfalls

Whether you are in the inner circle or outer circle of someone in crisis, walking alongside is an important role. To be most effective, it helps to be alert to potential pitfalls we may encounter.

For the **inner circle**, some of the most common pitfalls are:

❖ Trying to solve someone else's problem
❖ Trying to make someone else's decision
❖ Not asking for help
❖ Avoiding existing problems that surface

For the **outer circle**, some of the most common pitfalls are:

❖ Pulling away unnecessarily
❖ Mistaking your needs for theirs
❖ Mistaking your role

As you'll see, I fell into the last two traps in the story with Karen and Hal.

PITFALL: Trying to Solve Someone Else's Problem

When someone is in crisis, it is terribly tempting to want to "fix" things for him. If we can just solve his problem, then we all can get back to normal. Barring the type of emergency that requires immediate, external life-saving action, I would suggest it's more beneficial to help someone solve his own problems than to do it for him.

Pretend you are visiting the chiropractor three times a week for a back problem. The treatment is expected to last three months, and you're one month into the treatment. Which would you rather hear from your doctor?

❖ "I'm the doctor, and I know what to do. Plus I've got my staff, and they know what to do. Don't worry; you don't need to ask so many questions."
❖ "Let's take a look at what we've done so far. I've done technique A and technique B, and we've done things in this order and that order. What's working best for you?"

Maybe in the initial grips of shock, we would choose the first option. We are too lost to think logically and prefer to depend on others to make choices for us. But after the initial shock, most of us probably would choose the second option because it gives us a sense of control. A month into treatment, most of us would probably like to offer input.

A simple approach to helping someone solve his own problem is to ask:

❖ "What's working?"
❖ "What's not working?"

Then help him act accordingly.

PITFALL: Trying to Make Someone Else's Decision

Similarly, it can be tempting to make decisions for people in crisis. They may be indecisive. They may be confused. Again, I would suggest it usually is better to help those in crisis come to a conclusion on their own.

Here is a not uncommon situation: A woman is diagnosed with breast cancer. She has three options for treatment. She looks at her husband, "What should I do?" What if you, the husband, make the decision and things don't work out? As a result, your wife has to go back in for more surgery. Or has to add chemo to the mix. "You told me to do this, and look what happened!" What feelings of guilt or blame may arise?

And it doesn't have to be a spouse inappropriately making the decision. It could be another family member, a friend, or the trusted neighbor who drives the patient to the appointment.

Instead, if you are in the supporting role, ask questions, and listen to the answers. As much as possible let the person in crisis reach her own decision on how to proceed.

This might be a good situation to suggest bringing in a safe stranger, so the pressure on those closest to the person in crisis can be alleviated. It might be time to ask for help from someone with a level head and a good ear, who can sort, collate, and categorize information; someone who can present the information in a way that allows the person in crisis to come to a conclusion about her next step forward.

Remember, the further you are from the crisis, the easier it usually is to maintain some objectivity about the situation. The trick here is to find a balance between making someone else's decision versus offering insights based on your connection to that person.

PITFALL: Not Asking for Help

True to the meaning of his name Hyun-Ki Kim provided the "foundation of wisdom" for his family. As a young man, Mr. Kim immigrated to the United States from Korea to study engineering. He married an American woman, but they raised their only child, Chung-Cha, by Korean standards.

As the "righteous daughter," Chung-Cha was obedient, studious, and reserved. Brilliant like her father, she earned a scholarship to college and became a clinical researcher in pharmaceuticals. As she entered her career, Chung-Cha lived with her parents. When her mother died, Chung-Cha naturally assumed the role of keeper of the home.

As her father began to slide into dementia, Chung-Cha created safe ways for him to remain alone while she worked. At 6 p.m. each day she hurried home to cook, clean, and create activities to entertain her father the next day. In spite of his angry outbursts and frequent tantrums, Chung-Cha quietly coped with each worsening week.

Eventually, exhausted, Chung-cha began making mistakes at work. She found herself angry and resentful, emotions totally foreign to her. With her job in jeopardy, Chung-Cha reluctantly turned to her company's Employee Assistance Program (EAP) at her supervisor's insistence.

The EAP counselor helped Chung-Cha explore how she had handled stress in the past. Chung-Cha realized her family had taught her to keep problems at home and never to ask for help. Obviously this was untenable in the current situation.

To honor her cultural tradition and yet still cope with the current situation, Chung-Cha decided she was comfortable hiring some help, but not asking for favors. After a couple of tries, she found it was OK to hire someone to manage the housework but not the cooking.

Sometimes it's easier to seek help if we can figure out what specific type of help would actually make things better. That way we can feel true to our values without falling into the trap of martyrdom and exhaustion.

You may recognize the questions for reflection below from the Control chapter. They are just as relevant here.

QUESTIONS FOR REFLECTION

What is my pattern of asking for help? Do I? Don't I? When?

What's my comfort level with accepting help?

Would I prefer to pay for help or recruit volunteers?

What are the best- and worst-case scenarios if I go it alone?

If I don't get help, who will this affect?

Right now, what do I need help with the most?

PITFALL: Avoiding Problems That Surface

Ray and Vivian Walker's nineteen-year-old son Clay was arrested for driving under the influence (DUI). Fortunately he was stopped before an accident occurred. Driving to the police station they found themselves angry, embarrassed, and at a loss for words. A natural athlete, Clay had charmed his way through high school, made good grades, and landed a scholarship at a small college. Realizing it sounded silly, Ray said the only thing he could think of: "You know boys will be boys." But Vivian wasn't buying it.

They bailed Clay out, drove home in silence, and sat him down in the living room. Ray's approach was to let off steam fast, yell at Clay, and conclude with "Don't do it again!" Vivian knew this wasn't enough, but that was their final conversation about "the problem."

For weeks afterward, Vivian constantly sniped at Ray. In return Ray began stonewalling, speaking less and less as each day passed.

Vivian began thinking of divorce. How could she live with so much unhappiness? Ray began wondering how long he would have to keep walking on eggshells around Vivian.

Then Clay got another DUI.

Vivian and Ray realized that if they wanted to help Clay, they also needed to get some help for themselves. Their marriage already had some cracks in it; if they didn't get reinforcement, it would crumble.

Sometimes a presenting problem (such as Clay's drinking) makes visible a hidden problem (such as Vivian and Ray's communication). Like a fault line in the earth, the hidden problem has been there, but the stress of an earthquake (a crisis) makes it visible. Issues within marital relationships often happen around the illness or death of a child. In this case, Vivian and Ray were experiencing the "death" of "good boy Clay." If they'd left all the focus on Clay and his problems, they might never have addressed their deeper issues around values and communication.

In general, my advice is to pay attention to your gut; if something is bothering you, talk about it. Address the hidden problems that surface. Often (not always) when you work on that previously hidden problem, it can help improve the presenting problem. When you're in crisis and a hidden problem arises, it may be beneficial to get external, professional help from a therapist, counselor, or clergy member. An experienced, objective third party can bring the stability needed to address the problem productively.

QUESTIONS FOR REFLECTION

Have I encountered any of these pitfalls when supporting someone in crisis? What was the situation?

What would I do differently next time?

PITFALL: Pulling Away Unnecessarily

Have you ever felt yourself pulling away from someone in crisis? I have. And I've seen it happen frequently with people who have received a serious medical diagnosis, such as ALS or Alzheimer's, where they are "no longer themselves." Friends and colleagues don't visit or call; they seem to disappear. And it's not limited to illness. Why do we act this way?

Several common themes (spoken or unspoken) often are the culprits:

- ❖ "I don't know what to say, and I'm afraid I'll say something wrong."
- ❖ "I'm afraid this could happen to me too. Being around her makes me anxious and uncomfortable. It's too depressing."
- ❖ "I'm afraid I'll make the other person feel bad because I'm healthy [independent, employed, etc.]."

First, remember we're all human; we have emotional reactions that aren't always rational. The reactions above are completely normal; if you feel them, you're not alone.

Second, think about how many bad things you see happening every day. We can switch news sites or change channels, but we can't really avoid what is happening in the world. We remain aware of things that are not uplifting and happy. We also know that seeing something unpleasant doesn't cause it to happen. Just as reading news about a car crash does not cause a car crash, visiting someone with tremors due to Parkinson's disease doesn't increase our chance of getting Parkinson's.

Finally, we all make missteps (remember, we're all human), but an absence of connection can be worse than imperfect connection.

> *Even imperfect connections can be better than none at all.*

Put yourself in the other person's shoes: Would you want people pulling away, or maintaining connection? The answer may vary, but generally you will find that connection is preferred.

Connection can come in many forms: phone calls, cards and letters, personal visits. Since personal visits seem to cause the most anxiety, here's some practical advice.

- ❖ Realize that short but regular contact is sufficient. Pop in for five minutes when you're in the neighborhood; drop off a cup of coffee or a new magazine.

❖ You don't have to provide all of the entertainment. It's perfectly fine to watch a video or sports event.

❖ If conversation is a physical challenge, acknowledge the issue and your discomfort. "You know, Molly, I'm hitting a stumbling block here. You and I have always talked, but I know it's hard for you to talk now—and I'm not very good at monologs. Could this book be our in-between? How about I read to you for a bit?"

❖ Prepare for a visit. Preparation can decrease your anxiety. If you are more relaxed, the other person will likely be more relaxed, too.

❖ Take another friend along; visit as a tag team. The person you're seeing may enjoy a group visit, and the buddy system provides support for you. Just be sure to include the person you're visiting in the conversation, in effect if not in actuality.

One other question I ask myself when I find myself pulling away: "When this crisis is over, will I regret not being more involved?" This reflection often helps me push through any discomfort I may feel.

PITFALL: Mistaking Whose Needs You're Trying to Meet

When I was doing my chaplaincy training at a hospital, if a Code Blue (in other words, a life-threatening situation) was called, my job was to show up ASAP as part of the support team. Stand out in the hall. Comfort the family. Help with crowd control.

I felt so compelled to get there I would run. I would skip the elevator and take the stairs. I got there so fast that I acquired the nickname "Crash Cart Queen."

One day my mentor said, "Becky, you realize that's not exactly a compliment." Oh!

Was I really the first person who was needed on the scene? Maybe sometimes. But whose need was I really filling? Maybe I was filling *my need to be needed*. Maybe I was filling my need to be near the center of attention, in the spotlight. Hmmm.

I saw that pattern emerge again with Karen when Hal died. I wanted to rush to the hospital because I was sure I was "needed." If Karen were someone who was totally alone in the world or who had no resources, maybe I would have been needed. But I happen to know enough about Karen's life to know she has a church community. She has friends. She's not bereft and alone in the world. She certainly did not need to expend emotional energy trying to reconnect with someone she had not seen in many years.

From time to time, we all have the tendency to mistake whose needs we're trying to meet. If that's happening to you, consider the reflection questions below.

QUESTIONS FOR REFLECTION

Does the current situation connect intensely to a time in my own life? Do I have unfinished business with that experience?

Am I keeping an open mind about the true needs of the person in crisis? Or have I pre-determined what those needs are?

Am I helping the person in crisis look at all options available to help address needs or resolve issues?

PITFALL: Mistaking Your Role

Similar to mistaking whose needs we're trying to meet, we sometimes mistake the role we play in this situation. While I'd like to think that as inner and outer circle members we realize we are not the ones in crisis, sometimes we may still get that confused. But more often, outer circle members rush in as though they are members of the inner circle.

I nearly rushed to the hospital to "help" Karen. Luckily my friend's text message and my long ponderous walk helped me realize that Karen didn't need a face from the past barging in. While I was part of her inner circle twenty years ago, I was on the outer edge of her outer circle at this point; I needed to re-shape my actions and reactions to suit that role instead.

If you're unclear whether you are a part of the inner or outer circle for the person in crisis, consider the following reflection questions. Then, if you're still unclear about your role, you may need to simply talk to the person in crisis.

QUESTIONS FOR REFLECTION

What is my relationship with the person in crisis?

Has the person in crisis previously sought my help/advice?

What signals is the person in crisis giving me about my role?
- ♦ *Direct request for help?*
- ♦ *Request for resources but not for my personal help?*
- ♦ *Body language?*

What do I want my role to be?

Additionally we sometimes get mixed messages. For example, your neighbor has said he is under financial stress and may lose his house. You offer some advice about financial resources. He stiffens up, but asks another question. You feel confused by his mixed signals. It may be best to simply say, "I realize this is a sensitive topic. Is it helpful for me to offer ideas, or would you prefer I be a listening ear?"

A variation on the Platinum Rule: It doesn't matter whether you see yourself in the inner circle or outer circle; it matters *where the person in the bull's-eye sees you.*

How can you best be of help?

Throughout the chapters on the Four Cs of Stability we considered practical things you can do to help regain stability in the midst of crisis. In this chapter, we've looked at some tools to manage a crisis experience, and we've noted some pitfalls to avoid when helping others.

To decide how you can best be of help to someone in crisis, take a look in an intentional manner at when, where, and how you should be involved.

❖ **When** – Do you need to be involved immediately? Or can you be of more help next week when thing settle down? Or should you wait a few months for life to normalize, *then* say, "Hey, I haven't forgotten about you." Waiting might not seem as glamorous as being first on the scene, but in some ways, it can be even more nurturing.

❖ **Where** – Where is your presence best for the person in crisis? Are you truly going to be helpful at the hospital? Would you be more helpful while someone is in physical rehab and alone much of the day? Or when she is at home and can't quite manage everything yet?

❖ **How** – Besides showing up to offer comfort, are you able to contribute something else? Go back to the chapters on the Four Cs and look at all the practical things people in crisis can use.

During my walk to consider Karen's situation, I thought of things I could do that would be helpful to her and that would at the same time be comforting to me. I decided in the near term, I would send Karen a handwritten note and attend her husband's funeral. Down the road, when other people started to fall away or get tired, I would take her to lunch. *That's* when she would really need me. Taking her to lunch would offer her companionship and someone to talk to about her experience. And it would allow me to reconnect with someone who once had been central to my life.

> *Waiting might not seem as glamorous as being first on the scene, but it can be even more nurturing.*

We never know exactly what will happen when we offer our help to someone in crisis. Even with good intentions, we may step on someone else's pain. Even when offering comfort, we may remind them of something hurtful. It may be what we say, or don't say. It may be who we are, or who we aren't. We take a risk by allowing ourselves to be vulnerable when other people are vulnerable. Give each other the grace of forgiveness and understanding if things do not proceed as expected in a crisis.

HIGHLIGHT STORY: THE BIGGEST JOB YET

Larry Lytle had worked in technology most of his career, steadily navigating the industry jungle gym. He worked with Hewlett-Packard in strategic operations. He was hired by UNIX System Laboratories to prepare for a spin-out from AT&T. He was president and CEO of UnixWare Technology Group, a global consortium of high-tech companies.

When Larry landed at Nortel as VP of business development in Research Triangle Park, North Carolina, he loved it— so much so that he expected to be with Nortel until he retired. But then came the dot-com implosion, and his business unit was among the first casualties. Ultimately, Nortel itself declared bankruptcy.

Larry, ever resilient and resourceful, immediately embarked on his next mission as CEO of a struggling software company in Scottsdale, Arizona. The company had been after him for years, and their offer now looked pretty compelling. He agreed to a two-year contract and began a long commute.

When that obligation ended, Larry had the chance to try something completely new.

In 2003 Larry was encouraged by former-Governor Jim Hunt and several North Carolina business, education, and political leaders to serve as executive director of the World Trade Center North Carolina (WTCNC). The State had funded the WTCNC as a special economic development initiative, but never established it as a recurring line item in the annual budget. Since the center's funding wasn't stable, its previous directors had spent most of their time lobbying legislators and very little time on the mission of promoting North Carolina as a desirable place for global commerce.

The WTCNC had essentially died. It was quite literally reduced to a few boxes of files in a closet at NC State University.

Larry accepted the challenge to resurrect the WTCNC, revive its purpose and mission, find new sources of funding to sustain its operations, and build a strong brand identity. The salary was less than a third of that in Larry's previous job. The obstacles were enormous. Expectations were, at best, unsure. But Larry felt at his best in the midst of uncertainty and chaos with the odds stacked against him.

His entire life had prepared Larry for this job—yet nothing had. He realized his business acumen was crucial, and his ability to develop authentic relationships trumped even that. But he had no exceptional credentials, no specialized foreign policy or international trade experience.

What Larry did have was the willingness to go into a new venture without knowing the outcome. He'd done it before; he would do it again. And he *loved* it.

Larry thrived on developing relationships, on connecting people, on playing the negotiator, on advising businesses that wanted to expand internationally. Parts of the job were terribly exciting—hosting ambassadors and heads of state, visiting the White House and Congress, partnering with state departments and national organizations.

The satisfaction Larry found in this job translated into real business results for North Carolina, and he felt he was doing meaningful work. The center's board of directors regularly complimented him, and when they gave him a standing ovation for his accomplishments, Larry knew that his decision to embrace this challenge was the right one.

Then, suddenly, the job was gone. He wasn't fired. He wasn't even replaced initially. The job was just gone.

"I was riding pretty high in the saddle when suddenly I realized there was no horse under me," Larry said. "I truly felt betrayed. That gut-wrenching feeling of betrayal is probably the hardest thing I'd ever experienced."

An economic-development partnership had agreed to take over ownership of the WTCNC and provide the funding and staffing to assure its sustainability. Larry had been part of those negotiations and was led to believe he would continue to lead the center. But his successful turnaround efforts had made that position a nice plum. Larry's old job was given to someone else as a political favor—at double the salary.

Larry had been "Good Ol' Boy'd."

Before considering his next steps, Larry took time to reflect. He wondered whether he'd made mistakes. His evaluation was quick: not really. He hadn't messed up; he'd done well. Perhaps he was a bit overconfident and complacent; he clearly had missed some obvious political signals.

His next question was "What can I take away from this experience to strengthen me?" Out of a hurtful situation, Larry reaffirmed a core personal truth: "I am capable of reinvention. I embrace change. I am able to do incredible things and work with incredible people. I am content not being in a safe place all the time. There are always challenges needing someone to take them on. It is never too late to start again." In spite of everything, Larry knew the most important thing for him was continuing to develop honest, positive relationships.

He also realized that there were some things he couldn't fix. When that happens, he decided, you move on, find a new horse, and ride it with all the skill you have.

"It is never too late to start again...and again," Larry said. "Economic bubbles will burst. Funds sometimes dry up. Opportunities can disappear. Colleagues and friends may disappoint you. Seemingly solid careers may crumble. You've got to be resilient, adaptable, fearless, and the eternal adventurer."

That attitude is why Larry does not quietly go away. In recent years he has served as executive director of a business-development center in rural North Carolina and founder and president of the North Carolina Executive Roundtable. He continues to work with community college small-business centers to advise entrepreneurs launching new businesses; he teaches courses in personal branding, communications, and leadership; and he is the voice of the NC State Athletic Hall of Fame. Larry continually looks for new ways to help others succeed and make a difference.

Currently Larry uses his business, technology, and relationship-building talents working as chief strategy officer for his daughter's K-12 education software and services company. Together they help school administrators and teachers across the country make the transformation to digital learning.

Talk about authentic relationships and positive reinvention.

EXPERIENCE SUMMARY

Experience encompasses the conscious events that make up an individual life and the skill or knowledge obtained by doing something. In our car metaphor, experience is the frame of the car. It contains us, protects us, and offers a window to look through.

Whether our crisis is a difficulty, an acute crisis, a chronic crisis, or a life-altering change, we can use a series of questions to help us leverage past experience:

* ❖ Have I experienced **this situation** before? If so, what can I apply from that experience?
* ❖ Have I experienced **anything like this** before? If so, what can I apply from that experience?
* ❖ Is there anyone in my **inner circle** or **outer circle** that has had this experience or one like it before? If so, what can they help me learn about it?
* ❖ What else do I know that can help **mitigate the problem** even if I can't solve it?

In managing our crisis experience, we may find it useful to gather information, keep a journal, have someone else take notes for us, and talk to a safe stranger.

When helping someone else manage a crisis experience, it is important to keep in mind our own role as inner or outer circle and to act appropriately in that role. Common pitfalls include trying to solve someone else's problem or make someone else's decision, not asking for help, avoiding problems that surface, pulling away, and mistaking our role and whose needs we're trying to meet. To make sure we best meet the needs of the person in crisis, it helps to ask "When, where, and how can I be of most help?"

Assumptions:
Steering in the Right Direction

*We simply assume that the way we see things is the way they
really are or the way they should be. And our attitudes and
behaviors grow out of these assumptions.* —Stephen R. Covey

Rachelle Friedman was engaged and about to embark on a
new, married life. As fit and active lifeguards, naturally she
and her bridesmaids planned her bachelorette party at the
pool. As they horsed around, one of Rachelle's friends pushed
her in. Rachelle hit the bottom head first, broke her neck, and
suffered a spinal cord injury. Instantly, she became paralyzed,
quadriplegic.

Over the next year Rachelle not only went through physical rehabilitation, but she, her fiancé, Chris Chapman, and her
friends went through a sort of emotional rehabilitation. She
and Chris set themselves the goal of being the healthiest
people possible with the healthiest relationship possible; a
year later, they were married. Rachelle and her friends healed
and strengthened their relationships by muddling through
with sheer determination.

Rachelle now uses a wheelchair, but it would be inaccurate
to call her confined. Over the past several years, she has followed a dramatic course in her quest to become the most independent, healthy, vital young woman and wife that her
body will allow and technology will aid. She and Chris have
chosen to be very open about their situation. They've written a
book, *The Promise,* about their experiences and have shared

their story in multiple media venues. They're doggedly pursuing the cause of equipping and empowering people affected by spinal cord injuries. Along the way they're showing *everyone* how to create a rich life, even when snapped out of one reality and dropped into a new one.

Chris and Rachelle Chapman *knew* they would be loving parents, and at this writing they are rejoicing in the birth of their baby girl, Kaylee Rae, via surrogate mother, Laurel Hume.

WHAT DO WE MEAN BY *ASSUMPTION*?

Merriam-Webster offers the following definitions of *assumption*:
1. An assuming that something is true
2. A fact or statement (as a proposition, axiom, postulate, or notion) taken for granted

In the concept of assumptions, let's include perceptions, beliefs, and understandings. Of course, not all assumptions are true. But assumptions, true or false, underpin our worldview and our choices. Assumptions influence our actions during and after crisis.

In our car metaphor, assumptions are the steering mechanism. They determine our direction.

Types of Assumptions

In a very broad sense, we might say there are three main categories of assumptions:

❖ **Assumptions about yourself as a human** – Your value, capabilities, style, self-worth, patterns, and so on.
❖ **Assumptions about others** – How you view other people, what you believe about other people, how you expect other people to act.
❖ **Assumptions about the world around you** – How you view world events, your beliefs about work, philanthropy, causes, etc.

Where do we get our assumptions? From any number of places: our family of origin, our extended family, our religion, faith, or philosophy, our friends, peers, and colleagues, our schools and teachers, the media, the community in which we live, and on and on. We develop assumptions as a result of our life experience—what has happened to us and how we have interacted with others.

Different assumptions have different "stickiness." Some assumptions we hold rather mildly; if someone challenges us or offers new information, we are willing to change or discard that understanding rather easily. Other assumptions we may hold so deeply we don't even recognize them as assumptions—they are a part of our subterranean self, our "reptilian" brain. Some assumptions are top-of-mind, daily influencers; others appear only when we are in stressful situations.

The Value of Assumptions

Regardless of how positive Rachelle's assumptions are, they will not bring back her ability to walk. But assumptions *are* a major factor in how we experience a shock and how we process the shock after the fact. Rachelle's assumptions allowed her to take a positive, constructive approach in life-altering circumstances.

Clinical research has shown that assumptions and beliefs are indeed the *leverage point* on which our potential for dealing with a

> *Our success in moving forward from crisis hinges on our assumptions and beliefs.*

traumatic experience is determined. Will we fall backwards, get stuck, or move forward? In fact, post-traumatic growth (PTG) is a specific phenomenon in which a major negative shock leads individuals to significant personal growth and increased resilience. This occurs in large part due to their assumptions.

Our Assumptions Can Shape Our Actions

You find yourself about to be in a car crash (it doesn't matter whose fault it is). You are in that split second before impact where your instincts kick in. Do you tell yourself, "I'm a really good, savvy, defensive driver"? Or do you think to yourself, "I don't quite trust my reactions to be quick enough"?

If your assumption is "I'm a really good driver," there's at least a chance that the power of that assumption will trigger a good split-second decision. You are more likely to gain a temporary calm and an ability to see the situation clearly in that moment.

If you carry the assumption "I always panic" or "I always get into wrecks," there's a greater chance you *will* freeze up or panic or wreck.

Even in the midst of crisis, an assumption can precipitate a tiny difference that eases the situation, or worsens it. Those assumptions reside so deep within us that we're not making mindful decisions; we're simply listening to our unconscious guides in the moment.

Pop quiz: There's a scandal at work, and you have to speak publicly about it. Do you trust yourself to speak off the cuff? Do you tell yourself, "I'm a quick thinker. I know the right words will come to me"? Or do you say to yourself, "This is overwhelming. I don't do this well, and I will probably make a fool of myself"?

If you don't like your answer, keep reading.

We Can Shape Our Assumptions

When I talk about the power of assumptions in a crisis and the benefit of preparation, here's how the conversation often goes:

> Skeptic: "You don't know how you're going to respond in a crisis until you're in it, so you can't really prepare for it."

Me: "You're right, we can't prepare emotionally for every single possible crisis in life. Things happen. Let me ask you this: Do firefighters or police officers ever go through drills or training?"

Skeptic: "Of course they do!"

Me: "Why do you think they do that? Why would they waste their time doing that?"

The Skeptic's rather automatic response: "They're preparing to take care of people in an emergency. They're preparing to fight a fire or chase a criminal."

Aha! We can reasonably infer that there are ways in which we train ourselves so that *the necessary response becomes automatic within us.* Firefighters don't want to think about how to unroll the hose; they want their bodies to do it automatically.

We can take that same basic understanding and apply it to equipping ourselves for some of the emotional responses related to crisis. At any point, we can step back and become more aware of our assumptions. We can look at our guiding beliefs, whether they are helpful or harmful, and how they influence our choices.

The food we put into our psyche shows as clearly as the food we put into our bodies. Think about the way

> *Our psyche reflects the messages we feed it.*

we're raised and educated, the media impressions we receive daily, the messages that we hear over and over. Physical, mental, emotional, or spiritual, the things we choose to take in are the things that show themselves later.

If we can be more intentional about the beliefs and assumptions we hold, we have a better chance of moving forward with resilience when crises arise.

A METHODICAL APPROACH TO USING
ASSUMPTIONS TO DEAL WITH CRISIS

Throughout this book we've used the metaphor of a car to describe how the Four Cs and the E-A-R process fit together. We've described Assumptions as the steering or guidance mechanism for the car. Even with perfectly inflated tires (the Four Cs of Stability) and a beautiful exterior frame (Experience), unless we point the car in the right direction (Assumptions), it won't take us where we want to go.

Just as we talked in the prior chapter about assessing your own or others' experience, you can also look at your assumptions with a gentle yet discerning eye.

Let's continue our car metaphor. I've got things in the glove compartment that I've used to help me steer—maps, the GPS, scribbled directions on scraps of paper. Every once in a while I have to clean it all out. I might keep my North Carolina map because I use it on a regular basis, but the county map is out of date, so it needs to be replaced. And those scribbled directions? Toss them. My GPS, "Samantha," keeps taking me the long way; it's time to update her so she knows the new roads. Will I be going back to Georgia anytime soon? Maybe I'll throw that map in the trunk; I don't need it now, but I might want it later.

With our assumptions, we can use a similar methodical process:

1. Identify assumptions related to this situation or crisis.
2. Focus on two or three authentic, empowering assumptions.
3. Adapt or reframe assumptions to maintain authentic positive support.
4. Throw away or replace assumptions that are getting in the way.
5. Put some assumptions aside to look at again later.

Our goal is not to test every assumption we hold. Our goal is to use the power of our relevant assumptions in an authentic, positive way to support and strengthen us as we move through a crisis toward resilience.

Identify Your Assumptions

When I was in my late twenties, three years in a row I had a late-term miscarriage. The doctors gave me a variety of possible reasons, but they never could determine why those miscarriages happened.

The first time I miscarried, I started to hold within me the assumption that there was just something wrong with the baby; this was nature's way of causing the termination of a fetus that was seriously damaged. The second time, I took on the weight of an assumption that I had trouble carrying a pregnancy to term. Finally, I bore the burden of assuming I was simply incapable of having a full-term pregnancy. Because my husband and I strongly hoped to raise a child, this final assumption led to the decision to privately adopt.

We came within minutes of adopting a baby boy. As our attorney was about to enter the hospital room of the young mother, the baby's grandmother raced out.

"Nobody's taking this baby from our family. My husband and I will raise our grandson."

Only a few minutes later the papers would have been signed.

Bitterly disappointed, my husband and I stepped back to process what had just happened. How did we really feel about having children? What did we think about adoption? What assumptions were underlying our actions?

We affirmed that our first assumption was that we really, really wanted the chance to raise a child. Our second assumption was that we would be good parents, whether a child was born to us biologically or not. That was our guiding assumption.

After a few months, deep within myself I decided that I was capable of bearing a child, but somehow just hadn't done it correctly yet. I assumed, very consciously, that if we went about things differently, I would be capable of carrying to full term. I was a healthy, strong woman who wasn't even quite thirty years old at the time. Based on those two beliefs, without even consulting our doctor, we made the decision to go ahead and see if I could become pregnant again. I did.

After conducting my own positive pregnancy test, I called my obstetrician. He hadn't wanted me to get pregnant again because he thought it could be detrimental to my health, but he set aside his judgment. He rejoiced with us, and I never felt him being critical of us for taking that foolhardy step.

The doctor made his own assumption as well. Since there was nothing in the traditional medical records to explain why I'd lost those three babies, he assumed that I was simply a person who could not sustain a pregnancy during the normal rigors of everyday life. So he put me to bed. My assumption was that he was a wise doctor, so I followed his advice. At the end of the full term, I had a lovely, healthy baby girl, who was so happy in her little nesting womb that she had to be induced to come out.

In the twists and turns of life, assumptions guide our hopes and dreams. They cause us to take unconscious action and very deliberate action. Those actions sometimes work well, and sometimes they don't. In this particular circumstance, I'm happy to report they worked marvelously.

We can identify our own assumptions at any time, but it becomes more important in a stressful or shocking situation. Times you might want to consider your assumptions:

- ❖ Life is not going as expected. You are constantly shocked, surprised, or thrown off balance by events. What is your underlying assumption about how things are *supposed* to go?
- ❖ People do not act as you expect them to act. They react in unexpected ways. What is your underlying

assumption about how people *should* act? What are you assuming about *why* they are acting as they do?

❖ You must make a difficult decision. What factors are guiding your decision?

There are several ways you can identify your assumptions:

❖ Try what we did in the story above. Take a step back and ask yourself, "What do I assume about this situation?"

❖ Talk with a safe stranger. Sometimes another person can hear the underlying assumptions that you cannot recognize yourself. Be open to allowing that person to reflect what he hears from you.

❖ Listen to your gut. If something feels "right" or "wrong," why is that? What beliefs underpin your internal reaction?

By first recognizing our assumptions, we can then take the appropriate action with them—keep them, replace them, adapt them, or set them aside.

QUESTIONS FOR REFLECTION

Do I have a situation in which I need to assess my assumptions? What is the situation?

What are two to three important assumptions that are guiding me right now?

Common Places We Get Stuck in Our Assumptions

There are several common categories of assumptions in which we tend to get stuck. They happen across the board; they are not tied to any specific culture or religion.

• Presumptions about other people – What other people feel or believe; what other people will or will not do
• Negative or self-defeating beliefs
• Jumping to extremes of positive or negative, for example to either "you can't trust anyone" or "everyone is my friend"

Extreme Negative	Balanced Perspective	Extreme Positive
Things always go wrong	Many times things work out	Things always work out
The world's a terrible place	Many times the world is safe	The world is a safe place
You can't trust anyone	There are people I can trust	Everyone is my friend

Focus on Authentic, Empowering Assumptions

Our goal is to use the power of our assumptions in an authentic, positive way to support and strengthen us as we move through a crisis toward resilience. You probably already hold some authentic, positive, healthy assumptions related to the situation. You may call them beliefs or truths or assumptions; regardless, you can build on and strengthen them.

Choose two or three of those positive assumptions, the ones that you feel will do you the most good. Then try one or more of the following to maintain your focus on them:

❖ Use your positive assumptions as affirmations, especially in times of stress. "I have many friends and family who love and support me." "I have talents that can be applied to many different jobs." "People like to help me make new connections."

❖ Begin a gratitude practice. In your daily journal or before you go to bed at night, consider the positive things in your life and the positive true assumptions you hold; simply appreciate them. Research has shown that people who display more gratitude also demonstrate greater resilience, greater physical health, and greater mental health. In fact, gratitude may foster post-traumatic growth.

❖ Write your positive assumptions on notecards; post them where you will see them regularly.

❖ Include one or more of these beliefs into your regular conversation. This alerts the other person what is important to you and reinforces it in your own mind.

❖ Be aware of opposing beliefs as they come to mind. It's OK to talk to yourself. Try saying, "I know this negative assumption has come to mind. I choose to focus on _____ instead."

Use your positive assumptions to empower and equip yourself when in crisis.

Clara was one of the most headstrong ladies I ever met. She took up horseback riding in her sixties. She experienced a serious fall, had a leg amputated, and was told to prepare for a tough time in rehab. She told me, "I always pictured myself as vibrant and elegant on a horse. That's how I want to be on this new leg. My physical therapist may have a rough time with me, but I think I'll walk into my grandson's graduation in six months without any problems. I'm good at learning new things."

Guess what Clara did in six months.

QUESTIONS FOR REFLECTION

What am I grateful for in my life?

What positive, authentic assumptions do I hold?

What affirmations will support me right now?

Adapt or Reframe Your Assumptions

Sometimes we have an assumption that is empowering and affirming but may no longer be authentic, or vice versa: we have an authentic assumption that might not be positive. If these are important to our crisis or post-crisis situation, we may be able to adapt or reframe them.

Get Your Positive Assumption Another Way

Rachelle, from our opening story in this chapter, had thick, long, beautiful blond hair. Though she expected it to gray as she aged, she didn't expect it to change as a result of her accident. Unfortunately, one of the side effects of paralysis (related to blood flow) is a pronounced thinning of hair.

We all hold assumptions about our appearance ("I have great legs," "My nose is too big"). As subtle as they are, they are powerful. Now imagine you've lost the use of most of your body, much of your appearance is indelibly altered, and then one of your best features is diminished. Shock on top of shock.

But Rachelle did not want to give up her assumption of beautiful blond hair, so she got it another way—extensions. Rachelle was able to adjust her assumption in a way that maintained its positive truth. See Figure 12 for more examples.

Figure 12 Examples of Maintaining a Positive Assumption in Alternate Ways

Assumption	Previous Approach	Change	Alternate Approach
I am a prompt and punctual person.	I drive my car to appointments so I can be on time.	I lost my job and can no longer afford a car.	I plan carefully to take the bus to make my appointments on time.
I am a devoted wife and mother.	I cook and clean for my family and chauffeur my kids.	Injuries from a car wreck limit my activity.	I supervise meals and chores; I carpool with other parents; I listen to my family more.
I am a strong leader.	I listen well, think clearly, and reach conclusions easily.	Since my spouse's death, I can't focus.	I involve trusted staff in decision making to nurture their development.

To adjust your own assumptions, think through the statements in this process:

Statement to Yourself	Rachelle's Example
I assume [what empowering thing?] in this situation.	I assume I have beautiful hair.
This assumption used to be authentic by [what mechanism?].	This was true because I had naturally thick, long, blond hair.
I can no longer achieve this assumption because of [what change in circumstance?].	Due to my paralysis, my hair is thinning dramatically.
I can still maintain this assumption by [what different mechanism?].	I can still have beautiful, thick, long hair by using hair extensions.

If you get stuck (on the last step especially), try talking through the statements with a friend or a safe stranger to generate some ideas.

Address an Authentic Negative Assumption Positively

On the flip side, sometimes our assumptions are true, but have a negative impact on our lives if we let them sit there like stains on a rug.

Dahlia was in the midst of going through a divorce from her husband Marcus. She tended to be an introvert and did not like conflict. Marcus on the other hand was a charming extravert who treated life as a game; he loved to compete.

Dahlia's assumption in this situation was "I am not good at negotiations, especially in tense situations." Frankly, Dahlia knew that assumption was true—and she knew Marcus knew it, too.

Dahlia could have taken that assumption and continued with "I'm not good at negotiations, so Marcus will probably clean me out." This would be leaving the stain on the rug.

Instead Dahlia decided to use some situational "Resolve®." She extended her statement to "I'm not good at negotiations, *so I'm going to hire a really good attorney to speak on my behalf.*" Rather than wallowing in self-pity at her weaknesses, Dahlia decided to acknowledge this one and shore it up. Now she can authentically assume, "I am a competent, capable person looking out for my own best interests by hiring a competent, capable attorney." See Figure 13 for more examples.

Figure 13 Examples of Addressing an Authentic Negative Assumption

Crisis	Assumption	Leaving the Stain (Negative handling)	Using "Resolve" (Positive handling)
June's father needs in-home care, so comes to live with her family.	June has a low tolerance for noise and commotion.	June has angry outbursts with her family when the noise and chaos of too many people gets on her nerves.	June sets up a quiet corner in her home office where she can retreat to regain her calm.
Phillip's wife dies suddenly of a heart attack.	Phillip is a poor money manager. He and his wife have always managed the family finances together.	Phillip handles the family finances by himself; he can't sleep at night and worries that he and the kids might lose the house.	Phillip meets with a financial counselor; they analyze his budget and identify needed changes; they meet monthly until Phillip's confidence grows.
A job relocation takes Wesley from NJ to CA, where he knows no one.	Wesley finds it hard to make new friends.	Each day Wesley goes to work, returns to his apartment, and watches TV while he eats dinner. He begins to feel blue.	Wesley focuses on his love of soccer and joins a local team; eventually some of his teammates ask him to go out to eat after practice.

To address your own assumptions, think through the statements in the following process (and you know I will tell you to talk with a friend or safe stranger if you're getting stuck in a negative assumption):

Statement to Yourself	Dahlia's Example
I am informed by experience that [what skill, action, thing?] is important in this situation.	I am informed by experience that negotiation is important in divorce.
I assume that [what disempowering or negative thing?]. This is an authentic assumption.	I assume that I am not good at negotiation. This is an authentic assumption.
I have taken charge by [making what change or taking what action?].	I have taken charge by hiring a good lawyer to speak for me.
I can now adjust my authentic assumption to be "[what positive statement?] in this circumstance."	I can now adjust my authentic assumption to be "I am a competent and capable person in the divorce process."

Even with an authentic assumption that ties with a negative reality, we can bring it to a stronger, more resilient place.

Toss or Replace Assumptions That Are No Longer Useful

Sometimes our assumptions and beliefs are not life-supporting and empowering. The situation may have changed and the assumptions no longer hold, or the assumptions simply may not be beneficial. In this case we can either completely toss out our assumptions or replace them with more empowering ones.

Assumptions That No Longer Hold

During the economic turndown of the past several years, many people found themselves questioning their assumptions about work—they were laid off. Suddenly they no longer had a job to go to each morning. They no longer had a guaranteed paycheck in the bank on the first and fifteenth of the month. They no longer had the identity of "accountant at Green Manufacturing" or "IT project manager at Technical Systems, Inc."

I had the privilege of working with many folks who lost their jobs through no fault of their own. Some people learned about their job loss in dramatic fashion, some in tactless fashion (even via email or text!). Some had no indication their job was at risk. Some were in very high positions within their companies. Some had been employed fifteen, twenty, even thirty years *at the same company*. Some folks had never written a resume. They'd been hired straight out of college, and then were promoted or hired based on the results they'd gotten; they'd never had to go through another application or interview process.

Suddenly, they were dumped into the cold waters of unemployment, having to figure out not only "How do I paddle?" but "Where's the raft? Can I get on it? Will it hold all of us? Will we make it to shore?"

Obviously their assumptions about themselves, their skills, and their careers were being challenged. Some of their common assumptions might sound familiar to you:

❖ "I perform a very valuable job."
❖ "I have a valuable role, and I'll always be able to find a job in this role, even if it's with a different company."

Suddenly those assumptions were no longer necessarily true. Whether by technological displacement or corporate restructuring, many employees, including middle- and upper-tier professionals, had to replace those assumptions with a new one:

❖ "In the past, I performed a very valuable job; however, that role is no longer viable."

Then, in order to deal with this new reality, they had to take a serious look at deeper assumptions.

❖ "I'm good at only this type of work."

❖ "I have these skills or abilities, and that's it."

❖ "I work with these kinds of people, and that's what I'm best at that."

❖ "I work in this area of professional life and only this type of company."

❖ "I will always be employable by a firm. I'll always have benefits that go with my salary."

❖ "My savings and retirement plans will allow me to retire at XYZ date or have this many years of retirement."

At one end of the spectrum, people chose to close their eyes and say, "This is what's true. This is what's real. This is it." A few of those people were fortunate; they were able to land a position that fit with their previous assumptions and keep right on going. And of course more than a few were not so fortunate.

At the other end of the spectrum, people looked at their realities and their beliefs, and made huge shifts. Some decided their new assumption was "There's not going to be anyplace in traditional corporate life for my skills and abilities. I need to go into business for myself." Others decided they needed to go ahead and retire, and learn to live with the resources they had.

And all along the middle of the spectrum, other shifts took place. Many people said, "Whether I'm employable by another firm or find some way to create my own income, I need to look at some of my assumptions and see what I've got to do with them." Sometimes that meant retraining, learning new skills, or brushing up old skills. Other times it meant learning to craft a better resume, practicing interview skills, or strengthening a professional network. Those tasks and the willingness to work on them were fueled by the assumptions that people chose to strengthen, adapt, or politely put away.

To address your own assumptions that no longer hold, think through the statements in the following process:

Statement to Yourself	Layoff Example
My assumption until now has been [what?].	My assumption until now has been "I have a valuable role, and I'll always be able to find a job in this role, even if it's with a different company."
This assumption is no longer authentic because [what happened?].	This assumption is no longer authentic because the recession made my role a "nice to have" [or because manufacturing has moved to less expensive locations, or because new technology entered the market and my job is done by a machine now].
I need a new assumption that helps me [do what?].	I need a new assumption that helps me find a job [or generate income, or maintain my health benefits, or give me purpose].
My new authentic powering assumption will be [what?].	My new authentic assumption is "I have skills that are transferable to other industries and jobs" [or "I am smart and can take classes to learn new skills," or "My professional contacts want to help me"].

Assumptions That Are Disempowering

When thinking about assumptions to change, factual correctness is not always the issue. Subjective negative assumptions can be just as harmful as holding onto factually incorrect assumptions. For example,

- ❖ "I don't deserve to have friends; that's why no one ever calls me."
- ❖ "I'm horrible at relationships. I'll never be married."
- ❖ "I'm too old—no one will ever hire me."
- ❖ "I'll never make a good income."

These sorts of assumptions, which devalue us as individuals, deserve to be tossed out and replaced by positive, affirming assumptions. For example,

- ❖ "I have great friends who are glad when I call."
- ❖ "I will keep my eyes open for the right person to share my life with, but until then I will live life to the fullest."
- ❖ "I bring maturity and experience to the table."
- ❖ "I can find an employer who pays a fair salary for a job well done."

(Let me add a caution at this point. If after several months you find yourself staying "stuck" in a dark place and feeling only negative assumptions, even when you have support from friends and family, it might be time for a professional intervention. Talk to your family doctor or a counselor for an assessment of possible depression or other issues.)

Another common but disempowering assumption is "I don't have any choice." Frequently, this is our first reaction to a crisis situation. Rarely is it completely true.

Think back to Stephen Covey's 7 *Habits of Highly Effective People*. Habit 1 is "Be proactive." By that, Covey means recognize that you are free to choose and are responsible for your choices. You have a choice of action. You have a choice of response. You have a choice of emotion. You may not always have good choices—it may feel like you have to choose the lesser of two evils. You may have the choice of two equally good options. Or you may have a range of options. But the key point is, almost always, "I don't have any choice" is a false assumption.

Example: You are diagnosed with a terminal illness. You may have the choice of:

- ❖ Treating the pain so you are comfortable, or not treating the pain as aggressively so that your mind stays clear.
- ❖ Staying in the hospital with medical teams around you, or going home with your family, supported by hospice or a home health agency.
- ❖ Being depressed about your diagnosis, or taking every minute to enjoy the people and things you love.

Example: You lost your job. You may have the choice of:

- ❖ Actively learning new skills, or sticking to the belief you don't need to learn more.
- ❖ Asking for help from your network, even though it makes you uncomfortable, or crossing your fingers that all those online resume submissions will pay off.
- ❖ Taking a job that pays less than your last one so you can pay the bills, or dipping into your retirement savings.

Example: You are going through a nasty divorce. You may have the choice of:

- ❖ Talking trash about your ex- to your friends, or maintaining a neutral position.
- ❖ Driving a wedge between your ex- and your children, or trying to make the situation as positive as possible for the kids.

Some of these options may seem obviously "good" and "bad," but there is rarely such a stark dichotomy. Other options may be blurrier. It goes back to you and your situation. Just as the Four Cs are personal, the choices that are right for you are personal. The key is to hold assumptions and make choices that are empowering for you—while recognizing that other people may make a different choice.

I'm not saying it's easy. Life is tough. Life is not fair. At times, life stinks. Don't blame yourself for your initial reaction

"I don't have any choice." Instead recognize it as a reaction, then choose a more measured response to take you further down the path of resilience.

QUESTIONS FOR REFLECTION

What is a disempowering assumption that I hold?

What positive assumption will replace it?

Set Your Assumptions Aside for Later

In the healthcare world, I saw an assumption time and again that could be either extremely empowering or incredibly toxic: "When I am [sick, ill, in need], my [family, friends, church, club] will be there for me. They'll be steady, and I can count on them. Regardless of what happens, we'll get through this together."

When that assumption holds, there is almost nothing more powerful (though for some people, religious or spiritual beliefs may compare). When that assumption fails, it can be devastating.

Sometimes friends and family fall down in the support role from the very beginning, often from fear or uncertainty. Sometimes they wear out over time. Either way, the person holding that assumption is left without the resources he was counting on, and his very depth of trust is shaken. The people he assumed he could count on most did not live up to that as-sumption. It's a double whammy to resilience.

Sometimes the best thing you can do is gently set aside one of your assumptions. Don't keep it in front of you, but don't toss it out. Just package it up and put it on a shelf or in the trunk. Then, when the time feels right, take it back out and decide what to do with it.

In my experience, there are three main categories of assumptions that tend to get set aside:

❖ **Relationships** – Very often assumptions that need to be set aside are those relating to sensitive personal relationships, such as family members who have failed you. Do you need to forgive them? Forgive yourself? Do you need to end a relationship? Renew a relationship? The middle of a crisis is likely not the best place to decide.

❖ **Religious or philosophical beliefs** – In the Connection chapter we discussed some of the common responses to religion when in crisis. You may find your religion no longer offers solace. You may find the beliefs you held are now in conflict with your experience. You may want to run away from your faith. The middle of a crisis is likely not the best place to make those decisions.

❖ **Predictions** – After a job loss, people often jump to projections of their professional or financial future. They tend to drastically over- or under-estimate the situation. "I'll never be able to retire!" Again, the middle of a crisis is not a good time to make realistic assessments. Sure, there may be an impact, but deal with first things first. Look at the future when things have stabilized—*then* you are likely to be more accurate in your assessment.

When do you take tucked-away assumptions back out to review? Likely it will be after some time has passed and you are no longer in the immediate crisis. It may be when you are feeling stronger physically or emotionally. You might write down this assumption on a piece of paper, seal it in an envelope, and mark it with a specific date to look at it again. Or maybe you never do look at that assumption again.

Trust yourself to know when and how to address it.

Remember that you are in charge of your assumptions. Sometimes a small shift in them can equip and empower you for all kinds of new possibilities.

WALKING ALONGSIDE SOMEONE IN CRISIS

Just as we need to identify and manage our assumptions when we're in crisis, there are things that we can do when we are walking alongside someone in crisis. Three in particular stand out for me:

* Offer truth with kindness
* Hold open the door of possibility
* Test your own assumptions

Offer Truth with Kindness

When we walk alongside those in crisis, we may find ourselves judging them for their actions, their inactions, their emotions, their blind spots, or whatever it may be. At times when we feel judgmental, we may instead need to be kindly honest.

The Hebrew Scriptures say, "Let not kindness and truth forsake you. Bind them about your neck and write them on the tablet of your heart." (Proverbs 3:3)

We sometimes believe kindness and truth are at opposite ends of the spectrum and have no place in the same room. I don't see them as an either/or proposition. Indeed, I see them as being highly compatible. Allowing someone to continue in an untruth is not kind. Allowing him to continue in an untruth coddles him. Allowing him to continue in an untruth, in a way, treats him as a child rather than as an adult.

Victor approached me for guidance when he found that his job was coming to a sudden halt. He'd spent years honing his skills and building his reputation as a trusted and capable CPA. He'd handled major accounts and received excellent reviews on his work. Suddenly he found himself in a perplexing situation. After having what he thought were excellent interviews, he didn't understand why he wasn't getting called back.

During our conversation I realized that Victor's evaluation of his experience and his potential value to an employer was laced with his apparent assumption that his skills were unquestionably good. He saw himself as a very positive, self-assured person. Unfortunately, to the listener, this sounded like arrogance. (I was struck by the irony of needing to help a person tone down rather than pump up his self-assurance after a job loss.)

I made notes of several of Victor's exact statements. In a role-play where he was the potential employer and I was the candidate being interviewed for a job, I used several of his statements in describing my value. You should have seen the expression on his face. When I asked him what he thought, he laughed and said, "I think I understand why I'm not getting a second interview."

Bringing together truth and kindness may take creativity and emotional energy. But when you do it successfully, you give yourself and others the capacity to deal with reality and the potential for change.

Hold Open the Door of Possibility

Rachelle, the lovely young woman who was paralyzed in a pool accident, trained in college to be a recreational therapist. She'd worked with kids, she'd worked at the swimming pool, she'd worked at the senior center. She saw herself as a great "rec girl." She loved helping people have *fun*.

After Rachelle's accident, some of the people around her very gradually opened the door of possibility that Rachelle could become a voice for those affected by paralysis or other sudden life-changing trauma. As Rachelle began to consider this possibility, the people around her began to equip her for the challenge. Eventually, as she accepted this new role, Rachelle shifted from a cute, fun rec girl to a powerful, respected public speaker. By offering her voice to those who needed to hear it, she shifted from reaction to resilience and created a new deeply-held belief within herself: that even at a young age, she had a depth of wisdom to share.

Crisis limits our view of what's possible when the crisis is over. By making new possibilities visible to someone in crisis, we can help her transition away from reaction and negative assumptions and toward a positive future.

Holding open the door of possibility often is one of the privileges of the trusted friend or safe stranger; it may take some distance from the center of the crisis to see the possible positive outcomes. When you are in that role, recognize a few key points.

The person you're trying to help may not be thrilled about your help. Sometimes we can see all the potential and all the options for another person, and we want to fling that door of possibility open wide. But the person we're helping may not want that door open—or at least not yet. If you're feeling resistance, ask that person whether she wants you involved as a helper right now; if so, to what degree and at what pace? Let her say "I want you to be present, but quiet" or "I appreciate your caring about me, but I prefer to have someone else helping me with this part of things" or "I appreciate this; I'm just not ready yet."

It's one thing to open a door; it's another to push someone through it. When you hold open a door that displays many possibilities, avoid *preaching* those possibilities. Even caring, well-intentioned people find themselves falling into the trap of sermonizing. If the person you're talking to has closed her ears and is saying "Na na na na" (literally or figuratively), this may be exactly what's going on. It's OK to crack open the door of possibility for someone, and even to encourage her to walk through, but you can't shove her through that door.

We all tend to wear blinders. Sometimes we open the door of possibility and think we see the perfect answer. Then the person in crisis begins to move through the door, and she sees something else. She sees other possibilities—maybe better possibilities, or maybe just different possibilities. When opening the door for someone, be willing to not get tied to what *you* see initially. Be open to the emergence of other possibilities.

It can be important to invite other people into the process. Opening the door of possibility for someone is not a solo job. When helping Victor in his job search, the most important thing I could do was offer him the truth about his interview skills. But Victor also needed introductions to hiring managers within certain companies. I didn't have those relationships, but I could connect him to someone who did. Someone else was equipped to open that particular door wider than I could. Don't be afraid to ask for help.

Finally, I would offer the observation that sometimes in holding open the door for someone else, we begin to see new possibilities for ourselves.

Test Your Own Assumptions

We talked above about how we can open a door and see possibilities different from those the person in crisis sees. That mismatch in perceptions and beliefs extends beyond the door of possibilities. Even when you operate from a base of loving kindness, your assumptions may not match those of the person you are trying to help.

You may assume a situation is terrible; the person in the situation may see it as an obstacle to overcome, but nothing earth-shattering. You may assume there is only one good choice in this situation; the person in the situation may see something different as a good choice.

Recognize when there may be misalignment in assumptions. Ask about them directly if you can, and pay close attention to nonverbal signals. Consider the other person's:

❖ Assumption about what the **situation** really is
❖ **Emotions** around that assumption
❖ Assumption about what a good **outcome** looks like

Here's an example. As a hospice chaplain I played the safe stranger for many patients and their families. One of the protective, lovingly intended assumptions that families often held was along the lines of "We can't tell Grandma what's really going on. It will take away her hope if we tell her what her medical condition really is." Part of the hospice staff's role was to, as gently as we could, help the family understand how to separate their assumptions from Grandma's.

While it may not have been quite so linear, in essence we asked questions about the three points above to achieve understanding among family members (see Figure 14).

Figure 14 Example of How Assumptions Differ

	The family assumes:	Grandma assumes:
What's the **situation**?	Grandma doesn't know her medical condition; their role is to protect her.	She's been around a long time; she knows how her body feels, and she can make her own decisions.
What are the **emotions**?	Talking about Grandma's condition will take away hope and lead to despair.	Being able to talk openly will give her peace of mind.
What's a good **outcome**?	Having an honest conversation will be painful; avoiding the conversation will avoid the pain.	Having an honest conversation will allow her to say important things, make her own choices, and share a special closeness.

Families assumed they knew what was best for Grandma. While well intended, often they were mistaken. Likewise, any time we assume we know what others want or what is best for them, we may be mistaken. Remember the Platinum Rule: Do unto others as *they* want to be done unto.

QUESTIONS FOR REFLECTION

Am I walking alongside someone in crisis right now? If so, what is the situation?

What are my assumptions about the situation?

How do they align with the assumptions of the person in crisis?

Do I need to make any adjustments?

HIGHLIGHT STORY:
I WON'T TAKE THIS LYING DOWN

Jim Bankston describes his 1950s California childhood as "despairing." Not only was his father alcoholic, but after his parents divorced, subsequent step-fathers were as well.

From this despairing childhood, Jim learned many lessons. Two of the most important were "I will never treat people this way" and "I will not allow myself to be treated this way." In childhood Jim made a deliberate decision not to be a victim. This choice guided him into adulthood.

Along the way, Jim's education, faith, and friendships became his refuge. He earned multiple degrees, including a PhD, and discovered that his life direction was in human resources (HR). In that field he found he could use his understanding of the rules and regulations of the business world and also provide the tender care that was a part of his faith and personality. Jim now works fulltime as an HR manager and teaches HR, business, and research courses part-time in multiple undergraduate and graduate programs.

Jim sets higher expectations for his students than were sometimes set for him. On the first day of class Jim always says, "I expect all of you to finish this class." As he describes it, "Once a 'quitter' mindset takes root, it becomes increasingly easy to give up and accept failure as your lot in life." His students almost always finish the course.

Knowing the history of alcoholism and other health problems that plagued his family, Jim chose early on to maintain health patterns all doctors would wish for their patients: clean living, a healthful diet, and a positive outlook on life. In 2012 while treating Jim for a painful pinched nerve in his leg, Jim's doctor felt that more extensive tests were called for. To the surprise of both Jim and his physician, a CT scan showed a tumor anchored to the outside of Jim's kidney. Simultaneously a mass was found inside his lung.

Jim's surgeon ordered immediate surgery. When Jim said, "No, I need to finish teaching this class," the doctor reluctantly acceded to his wishes. One more week *probably* wouldn't hurt... Jim felt strongly he needed to abide by the same expectation he'd given his students; he couldn't let them down.

Jim sat out on his porch that night and reflected on the situation. After about twenty minutes, he got up and said in a calm, but determined voice, "OK, you bastard, it's on."

The day following the last class of the semester, Jim was rolled into surgery. But before that, he made one request: other than being on the operating table, at all other times, he wanted to be in a recliner, not a bed. Lying in bed symbolized giving in to the cancer, and he was not giving in. He was going to be in control. The doctors agreed.

As Jim went into surgery, the doctors weren't sure whether Jim had two separate cancers or whether the kidney cancer had spread to his lungs. The latter would be worse. Though it was ultimately determined there were two separate cancers, Jim later learned his type and level of cancer carried only a fourteen percent survival rate.

Jim believed his clean-living lifestyle would place him in that fourteen percent—with a little luck and God willing.

During his treatment, Jim realized cancer had been in his body for five years. "The cancer just hid," Jim says. "I was the one who fought. Cancer was a coward; it wouldn't even engage in a fair fight. Anger kept me from being depressed, and faith kept me from being afraid. Most people are looking for God to bail them out. I think God puts you in the boat and expects you to row. And as long as I have life, I assume that I'm supposed to live this life."

As of the writing of this book, Jim is three years post-surgery. The doctors told Jim that by making it to the two-year mark, he was well within that fourteen percent. Jim smiled. He knew he'd given cancer the best fight he could.

It appears he is winning.

ASSUMPTIONS SUMMARY

Assumptions are those things we take for granted as true. We may also call them perceptions, beliefs, or understandings. They may or may not be factually true, but they underpin our worldview and our choices. In our car metaphor, assumptions are the steering or guidance system.

The assumptions we hold about ourselves, about others, and about the world around us come from many sources: family, friends, faith, media, schools, community. Our assumptions shape our actions. If we can learn to shape our assumptions, they can more effectively serve us.

In crisis our goal is to use the power of our assumptions in an authentic, positive way to support and strengthen us as we move through a crisis toward resilience. We can use a methodical process:

1. Identify our assumptions related to this situation or crisis
2. Focus on two or three empowering authentic assumptions
3. Adapt or reframe authentic assumptions (positive or negative) to maintain authentic positive support
4. Throw away or replace assumptions that are getting in our way
5. Put some assumptions aside to look at again later

When we walk alongside those in crisis, our role is to help them assess and use their own assumptions by offering truth with kindness and holding open the door of possibility, while not letting our own assumptions get in the way.

Resources:
Taking Stock

*Life is constantly providing us with new funds, new resources,
even when we are reduced to immobility. In life's ledger there is no
such thing as frozen assets.* —Henry Miller

Hector had held an executive position for many years. One day, as a result of the recession and restructuring, his position was eliminated. He couldn't believe his colleagues had kept him in the dark while they schemed around him. He was humiliated. He couldn't tell his family.

The morning after he was laid off, he got up, put on his suit and tie, got his laptop bag, and went out the door at the regular time. He sat in a coffee shop and tried to figure out what to do. The following day he did the same. After a week, he realized he couldn't lie to his wife anymore. But even after he confessed to her, he couldn't reveal his situation fully to the world, and he continued in his daily coffee-shop visits.

Hector struggled with what would happen next, but because he was a methodical person, he sat down and made lists of who to contact and things to do—the standard jobseeker activities. He found out how to access his company's outplacement program. He looked into the Employment Security Commission. He updated his resume.

He took all those logical first steps and felt pretty secure about how he was using his resources, his intellect, his common sense. Then, a few weeks down the road Hector hit a piece of reality that he'd missed before: he was expendable. He was used to being a resource, and now he was suddenly not needed. Hector had found himself not only without a six-figure income, but without anything to do on a day-to-day basis. He found himself without purpose.

Hector bumped into a buddy at the coffee shop one Thursday morning.

"You know," his buddy said, "I think I'm in the same spot you are. We're both sitting here at ten o'clock, and we've both got our briefcases and we're both in our coats and ties—and we're not on a job."

Hector kind of laughed with some embarrassment and said, "Yeah."

"Well," his buddy said, "I've got someplace that I need you to be tomorrow morning, but I don't want you to be in a coat and tie. Just wear jeans and a flannel shirt." He handed Hector the address. "Be there about ten o'clock tomorrow morning. I really need you to show up."

The next morning Hector plugged the address into his car's GPS, which directed him toward the inner city. He found a place to park, walked to the exact address, and realized he was approaching the back door of a soup kitchen. That day, and over the course of the next few months, Hector volunteered with a group of men who served meals and encouragement to homeless men.

This volunteerism became a resource that allowed Hector to tap back into his assumption that he served a purpose. Hector realized that serving these men, sitting down with them for coffee, finding commonality with them as human beings, opened up a whole part of himself that he didn't know was there.

As it turned out, Hector ended up looking for a different type of job from what he had initially intended. He ended up working as an executive in a non-profit organization and was able to bring his corporate experience to that setting.

By looking at his own personal experience and by testing his own assumptions about his career, Hector was able to use his resources to make a career change that brought him greater meaning and purpose. That's how these pieces — experience, assumptions, and resources — can start to come together.

WHAT DO WE MEAN BY *RESOURCES*?

Merriam-Webster offers several definitions of *resource*. Three of the most appropriate to our discussion include:
1. A source of supply or support
2. A source of information or expertise
3. Something to which one has recourse in difficulty

Recall in our car analogy we described resources as the fuel that powers our vehicle. We can have all the parts and pieces (our Four Cs, Experience, and Assumptions), but without gas, diesel, or a battery (Resources), we can't move.

Types of Resources

When we say "resources," for most people physical, tangible items pop to mind. Let's look at some of those, as well as at some resources that might not be so obvious.

Physical Resources – We live in a physical world, so we quickly pay attention to resources that we can see and hear and taste and touch — all the easily identifiable things that make life function.

- ❖ Food – Anything from basic sustenance to fancy food to comfort food
- ❖ Shelter – Housing and all the things that go with it, such as furniture and utilities
- ❖ Clothing – The right clothing, clean clothing, enough clothing
- ❖ Electronics – Laptop, smart phone, iPod, big-screen TV (the list is endless…)
- ❖ Medical treatment – Prescriptions, surgery, rehab, chemotherapy, dialysis, and so forth

❖ Transportation – A car or bike; access to the bus or
subway or other public transportation

Financial Resources – Many people get uncomfortable
talking about money or perhaps feel superficial that money
springs to mind so easily, but financial resources are important on a daily basis and during crisis. They may include:

❖ Income
❖ Savings
❖ Retirement funds
❖ Investments
❖ Insurance

Social Resources – "Social" resources can take many different forms.

❖ Friends and family – We need people who are kind,
caring, supportive, and consistent in their interaction.

❖ Spiritual family – People of faith need clergy and
others to pray for them and offer spiritual support (not
to mention bring casseroles!).

❖ Professionals – We need people who provide legal,
medical, financial, business, counseling, and many
other specialized services.

❖ Connectors – We may need people to help us find
professional help or resources to move us through this
crisis.

Internal Resources – Sometimes we forget we can call on
our own inner strength as a resource; other times we may
think that is the only resource we have.

❖ Our own personal makeup – We all have positive
attributes that can help us through crisis: confidence,
flexibility, calmness; even characteristics like anger and
stubbornness.

❖ Our personal experience – We spent an entire chapter
on experience. Recognize that the totality of your
experience (family, education, social setting, etc.)
contributes to who you are and how you handle

disruption and crisis. Don't forget it can be an emotional resource as well as a practical one.

❖ Our spiritual or philosophical base – We spent some time on this topic in the Connection chapter and to some extent in the Assumptions chapter. Recognize also how your core values (religious or non-religious) can be a resource for you in disruptive times.

The Value of Resources

It doesn't require mastery of Maslow's hierarchy of needs to know that our lives depend on resources. From as basic as clothing, food, and shelter to as advanced as the technology that rules our days, resources determine not only whether we will live or die, but in what condition.

In much of our life, we determine the significance of a resource. It could be absolutely crucial or entirely expendable.

In crisis, our resources often determine how quickly we stabilize and begin moving toward resilience. For example, if you're reasonably healthy, break your leg, and don't get medical care, your leg probably will heal and you eventually will walk, but you may be disfigured or have a lifetime of pain. In that same situation, if you get medical care to set the leg, put it in a cast, and help you through rehabilitation, chances are you will not only walk but will get back to your pre-break "normal."

Resources often determine how quickly we stabilize and begin moving toward resilience.

Resources can make our crisis journey faster and smoother, but only if we have access to them and make use of them.

Resources Are Individual

We know that when we're in crisis, we all react differently. While we have a commonality in that we all have our four Cs, the way we approach them is different. The rate at which we move out of a reactionary place is likewise specific to each person. Additionally, the assessment of resources we have and resources we feel we need is unique to each person.

> *Each experience requires different resources.*

Let's say the business where you work is engulfed in flames. Suddenly everything has stopped for an undetermined period of time, and the owners aren't sure how they're going to make payroll. Consider the different reactions you might get from:

- ❖ Gloria, who feels she has adequate resources to live life, has people around her, and has meaning and purpose within her.
- ❖ Frances, who's a single mom holding down two jobs just to make the rent and the car payment, while worrying that her abusive ex-husband is about to show up at the door.

These two individuals certainly bring different resources to the table.

The irony is that Gloria, who appears to be well resourced, may carry childhood trauma with her from the night that she was at Grandpa's house and it caught on fire; Gloria was terrified but had to jump out the window into the firefighter's arms. And Frances, who appears to have very little stability in her life, may come from an exceptionally strong base of coping. Perhaps her mother was a rock who instilled in her that it doesn't matter what's happening around you, you're a strong woman, and you can do whatever you must. Frances may have an internal resource that's far beyond what's seen in her checking account.

Visible, invisible; past, present; tangible, emotional. All of these relate to the role of resources in our lives. Yet, one more defining aspect may override all of the others: perception vs. reality.

Perception vs. Reality

Long ago there was an old Japanese woman who wished to know the difference between Heaven and Hell. The monks in the temple agreed to show her. They took her to a wall with two doors.

They opened the first door and said, "This is Hell." The old woman saw many people seated at a long table filled with the finest foods. But the people seated at the table looked gaunt and distressed. She looked more closely and saw each of their hands had only two fingers shaped like *hashi*, Japanese chopsticks—four feet long! Their fingers were *so* long they could not get the food into their mouths.

The monks opened the second door and said, "This is Heaven." The old woman again saw many people seated at a long table filled with the finest foods. Their hands, too, were shaped like four-foot-long *hashi*, but these people had plump cheeks and smiles on their faces. She watched as a young boy picked up some rice and vegetables, reached across the table, and said "Here, sister, try this!"

Just as in this allegory, which has many variations across cultures, the same situation can be handled in different ways and lead to different results—happy or sad, fed or unfed. Some people find themselves in crisis with a great deal of resources—or their own *perception* of a great deal of resources. Other individuals have tremendous resources as the world views it, but they don't see themselves that way. Particularly in crisis, our perception can become skewed. This is one reason I encourage you to look at your assumptions before you look at your resources.

A METHODICAL APPROACH TO
MANAGING OUR RESOURCES

In the last two chapters we talked about understanding our experiences and assumptions in the context of a particular crisis. The third step is to assess the resources needed and the resources at hand for handling the situation.

The whole E-A-R process is:

1. **Experience** – Consider your experience (or that of those around you) relative to this situation. How can you use it?

2. **Assumptions** – Look at your assumptions and beliefs relative to this situation. Which should you keep, adjust, or put away?

3. **Resources** – Based on the above...
   ◆ What resources do you have?
   ◆ What resources do you need?
   ◆ What resources do you need to *learn to live without*?

It's easy to jump right to resources. (Remember the image of spraying gas on the car parts?) But by assessing our experience and assumptions first, we may find we need different resources from what we thought originally. I've also learned from many individuals that the resources needed in the moment of crisis are often different from those needed further down the road.

When you are in the immediate blast of a crisis, you focus on the most urgent resources for that point in time.

   ❖ In a car crash, you get medical attention and a tow truck to get the car off the road.
   ❖ In a house fire, you get the fire department to put out the fire.
   ❖ In a heart attack, you get to the hospital for medical treatment.

After the shock, you look at the need for longer-term resources.

❖ After the car crash, you assess responsibility and deal with legal issues with the other driver. You talk to the insurance company to determine what is covered and learn about implications for your insurance rates. You deal with any longer-term physical issues as a result of injury. You may need an attorney, money for car replacement and medical bills, a physical therapist, or a therapist for emotional trauma.

❖ After the house fire, you work with your insurance company to determine whether the house can be rebuilt, where you are going to stay, how you are going to replace your belongings. You may need knowledgeable contractors, temporary housing with family or in an apartment, money for replacing your belongings if your insurance doesn't cover everything, and time off work to manage all the moving pieces.

❖ After the heart attack, you work with your doctor to develop a health plan. You make changes to your diet, your exercise, and your work routine. You may need a personal trainer or a gym membership, ongoing medical care, a housekeeper to keep order while you recover, lengthy time off from work, and so on.

Of course you need those immediate emergency resources, but don't forget about the importance of the longer-term resources. The immediate resources are needed during the initial response to a crisis, and the longer-term resources help on the path toward resilience.

Let's look at the Resource process in more detail.

What do I have? What do I need?

What do I have? and *What do I need?* are two sides of the same coin. Part of the movement toward resilience entails looking more clearly at these two questions. By first reviewing our experience and assumptions, we have better context and broadness of perspective in answering them.

Crisis can erase our memory of what we *do* have, leaving us feeling needy. In dire circumstances, a person might lose absolutely everything—health, home, family, and funds. Most of the time, however, even a serious crisis spares at least one of these resources.

If you feel stumped trying to figure out what resources you do have, ask a friend or safe stranger to help you list several of your key assets. Even if these resources strike you as obvious or unrelated to your current situation, this exercise will do two things:

1. Provide you with specific reminders of your resources. They might come in handy later even if they're not needed now.

2. Stir feelings of gratitude within you. Gratitude is a resilience-building factor.

QUESTION FOR REFLECTION

What resources do I have, even if they don't seem of obvious use in my current crisis?

On the flip side, crisis may create a need for new resources.

In an initial reactive situation, we often need something that we already have quickly at hand or that can be handed to us immediately. That's appropriate, because you're not in a situation where you can ponder or reflect. If you've fallen and gotten hurt, you get your first aid kit and grab the sterile pads, antibiotic cream, and bandages. Likewise when someone suffers a loss, you show up with that pie or a casserole quickly (even if it has to be frozen to eat later on). You bring something that says in tangible and emotional ways, "I'm here for you. I'm here to help."

One of the ways that we can tell that we're starting to move through the resilience-building continuum is when we can move to the next layer of depth. If we continue the example of falling and getting hurt, we might realize we need a few things outside the first-aid kit. Perhaps we need a tetanus shot or stitches to heal properly.

Similarly, in crisis, we can consider some of the possible resources we might need during and just after a crisis, as well as resources we need longer term (see Figure 15).

Figure 15 Sample Short-term and Long-term Resources

Situation	During this crisis I need:	Longer term I need:
Death of best friend	People who understand how significant this loss is for me; books that are written specifically about the loss of a friend (rather than spouse or family)	Strong, positive memories of my best friend that can be talismans as I start new friendships or deepen existing ones
Emergency adoption of teenage nephew	Clothing, personal items, and room for my nephew; an attorney for legal matters; information about school arrangements	A family counselor to help us with adjustment and emotional issues related to the reason for adoption; a support group for adopted children and parents of adopted children
Job loss	Funds from savings or other source; a good resume	A mentor; a system to record my professional accomplishments for the next time I change jobs
Family member dealing with drug or alcohol abuse	A detox or rehab facility; medical and/or psychological care for my addicted relative, my family, and myself; an attorney so we understand any legal implications; funds to cover all these expenses	Ongoing counseling or support groups like Alcoholics Anonymous or SMART Recovery; guidance in developing new life patterns, possibly including making new friends or learning not to be co-dependent

---

QUESTIONS FOR REFLECTION

*What resources do I need in my current crisis? Short term?
Long term?*

Which resources do I already have?

What do I need to learn to live without?

Professional ballroom dancer Adrianne Haslet-Davis lost
the lower half of her left leg in the Boston Marathon bombing.
Determined to dance again, she focused her rehabilitation
efforts on accepting her current reality while planning for a
future that still included dancing. Thanks to the intervention
of Hugh Herr of the Biomechatronics Group at the MIT Media
Lab, himself a double amputee, Adrianne would reach her
goal. Hugh and his team studied the elements of dance and
created a bionic prosthetic specially designed for Adrianne.
Less than a year after the bombing, Adrianne Haslet-Davis
performed a rumba with a dashing dance partner at the Van-
couver TED conference. Her swirling, sequined short skirt
showed one original leg and one brand-spanking-new leg con-
structed of metal, hinges, and microprocessors. And, boy, did
she dance.

When people experience something as dramatic as an am-
putation, it's very clear that a natural limb is not coming back.
Thanks to the wonders of technology and medicine, wedded
in some very unique and exciting ways, modern prosthetics
can allow tremendous mobility. They open up opportunities
for movement and agility that were completely unforeseen

twenty-five and definitely fifty years ago. But they are still prosthetics. That arm or leg or hand, at least at this stage in our technological advancement, is not coming back.

Thinking of that example, it's appropriate to consider what is not coming back in our life after a crisis. *What do I need to learn to live without?*

Sometimes the answers are obvious. I have to live without the limb I lost. I have to live without a loved one who died. I may have to live without my ex-husband's family because of our divorce.

Sometimes we have to learn to live without things that are not so obvious. I lost my job and had to change cities to find new work. As a result, I also lost my network of friends and colleagues, my familiarity with the geographic location I'm in, and the clubs and organizations I've been part of. While I can rebuild some of those things, I have to live without them for the time being. See Figure 16 for more examples.

After a crisis, a natural part of our emotional being numbs us to a loss for a period of time. Some call it Pollyanna thinking; some call it denial. In my experience, our emotional Novocain kicks in until we can start to grasp that we are not living in the midst of a bad dream. As reality dawns on us, we come to grips with the lack of this resource in our lives. How will we reframe in order to move to a healthy place, albeit a different one?

Figure 16 Sample Obvious and Less Obvious Losses

Situation	Obvious Loss	Less Obvious Loss
Job lay-off	Loss of income	Collegial relationships
House fire	Loss of shelter	Memories, a sense of "home"
Being robbed	Items stolen	Sense of safety, time needed to retrieve information and protect against identity theft
Becoming the caregiver for a sick or elderly person	Time, freedom	Mental stimulation, fun, flexibility, sleep

QUESTIONS FOR REFLECTION

What are my areas of loss? Obvious? Less obvious?

What are ways to fill those losses?

Who can help me with filling those losses?

WALKING ALONGSIDE SOMEONE IN CRISIS

My husband was coming home from the hospital after an extended stay at a physical rehabilitation facility to recover from his stroke. As we pulled up to the drive, I suddenly noticed that the lawn had been mowed—and not by me. Matter of fact, I didn't even know *when* it had been mowed. While I was out that morning? The day before? I had been too preoccupied with my husband's homecoming to notice!

Some simple detective work led me to the next door neighbor. My husband was a thirty-four-year-old man barely able to take care of himself, let alone the yard. That neighbor provided a resource to us that didn't make the headlines in the newspaper, but certainly made a headline in our life. Thirty-some years later, I still think of that neighbor with gratitude and affection.

We all can be a resource to someone who is going through a crisis. We can:

❖ Observe what's needed
❖ Ask what's needed
❖ Offer the resources we have

You may wish to refer back to the four crisis quadrants (difficulty, acute crisis, chronic crisis, life-altering change) as well as consider whether you are a member of the inner or outer circle of the person in crisis to determine what's most appropriate.

Observe What's Needed

Our neighbor simply observed what we needed and provided it. Now, without intentionally trying to play into sex-stereotyped roles, it was pretty clear in our household that my husband had been the yard worker and I had been the house-cleaner. Our neighbor could easily see that and knew us well enough that he felt comfortable cutting our grass without asking. While not all tasks lend themselves to that approach, mowing the lawn and shoveling the walk are fairly straight-forward and unobjectionable.

If you don't see anything as obvious as shaggy grass, try visualizing yourself in the crisis-afflicted person's situation. See his home, family, vehicles, job, and anything else you know about his life. Picture his typical day. Then picture what you know about his life in the midst of this crisis. Use the questions for reflection below to get started. By stepping into the other person's world, you may discover a variety of ways to provide what's needed.

QUESTIONS FOR REFLECTION

Are there pets, children, or other dependents who may need transportation, supervision, or special attention?

Does anyone need:
- ♦ *A "comfort kit" during a hospital stay (whether as a patient, family member, or friend)?*
- ♦ *A travel kit for an emergency trip?*
- ♦ *An extra guest room for a few nights?*
- ♦ *Something cheerful, distracting, or humorous?*

Are there roles that someone needs you to fill? (I record the attendance for a group every week. Imagine my delight when I returned after a month-long emergency to find all the records up to date!)

Ask What's Needed

If you can't observe the things that need doing, ask. Ask the person in crisis if possible, but remember you may need to ask a spouse, family member, or friend if that person is unavailable. When you ask, consider the Four Cs (Comfort, Control, Community, and Connection).

Focus on practical things, and ask specific questions (remember how hard it is to focus and think in a crisis). Use the previous exercise of putting yourself in the other person's place to distinguish areas where you can provide the best resources. For example, you might be very helpful with work-related needs, but not with childcare. Remember also that you may serve as a connector to needed resources. Sometimes the act of asking a thoughtful question triggers an idea for the person in crisis.

If asking too many questions makes you uncomfortable, try this technique: Say "I was wondering if…"

❖ "you might need…"
❖ "you might want…"
❖ "you might find useful…"
❖ "it might make things smoother at work if I were to…"

Remember that sometimes the recipient may not show great enthusiasm. Often she is overwhelmed, frightened, grieving, or angry. Giving you permission to do something may be all the communication energy she can muster. Sometimes you might hear "You can if you want to." Go ahead and "want to" for both of you.

Offer the Resources You Have

In our discussion of assumptions, I recounted my experience with three miscarriages. At the time, my husband and I lived in a very small town, and while people were very helpful and loving, they were also very *present*. You just couldn't hide *anything* in a town of a thousand people.

Shortly after one of my miscarriages, friends offered the use of their beach cottage. "It's not fancy, but we'd be glad for you to use it for a weekend or a week, whatever you need, just to get away by yourselves."

At the time, we thought what we needed was having everybody around us because we were so devastated, but we felt compelled to accept this kind offer. We intended to go for just a couple of days, but found something unexpected at their beach cottage. Having time totally apart from the community members, no matter how wonderful and loving they were, allowed us to start breathing again. It allowed us to start getting back on our feet after our shock. We ended up staying for five days.

We didn't even know we needed that particular resource, let alone the depth to which we needed it. The interesting thing was, our friends didn't see their offer as any big deal. It was off-season; the place wasn't rented. They just casually mentioned it. Sometimes it doesn't take great philosophical thought or great psychological awareness; sometimes just offering the things we have can be enough.

The resource you provide may be valuable or inexpensive. It may be creative or mundane. It may be difficult to obtain or easily at hand. Regardless, if it's a resource that's needed and provides any of the Four Cs, it can have a huge impact not only at the moment, but far down the road.

> *Sometimes it doesn't take great philosophical thought or great psychological awareness; sometimes just offering the things we have can be enough.*

HIGHLIGHT STORY: REACHING FOR THE STARS

Sharon Giovinazzo served her country as a combat medic in Desert Storm. After she returned from deployment, she began having trouble with her vision, but, always stubborn, she avoided the doctor until it worsened enough to annoy her. While driving to the doctor's office, she noticed trouble distinguishing stoplights and street signs. When the doctor asked her to read the eye chart at end of hall, she realized she couldn't even *see* the chart.

A series of tests revealed Sharon had multiple sclerosis (MS). If the doctor had been able to catch the MS earlier, it may have been possible to mitigate or reverse her vision problems, but Sharon's stubbornness came back to haunt her. Within six months, she became totally blind.

This tenacious woman took many classes to learn how to remain independent, and she began working for an organization that served people with sight and hearing challenges. When she learned that a state agency offered vocational educational assistance for those with disabilities, she registered at the local community college to pursue her undergraduate degree.

In Sharon's work, she frequently found herself lobbying on behalf of her clients. Recognizing her passion for advocacy, the CEO created a new public policy role for her. Her employer also helped her get into business school, so Sharon completed her undergraduate degree while working full time and beginning a "mini-MBA."

Eventually Sharon moved to a position in a workforce development agency. While there, she worked on a project for the deaf and blind in rural Kentucky. During a series of interviews with the project's constituents, she talked with a woman named Loretta Lynn, who was a coal miner's daughter (no joke). Loretta was legally blind, but retained some limited light perception. Sharon at one point asked her, "If there was one thing you could do, what would it be?"

Loretta responded, "I've never seen the stars, and it hurts my heart."

Over the course of the day and fifteen more interviews, multiple people independently said the same thing: "I'd like to see the stars." Sharon realized that in her thirty-one sighted years, she had been blessed to see the stars many times. She knew she had to help these people see the stars too. She wasn't sure how, but she had an idea that technology could help.

After researching the possibilities, Sharon gathered these nearly blind people on a big front porch after dark. Behind each visually impaired person stood a sighted professional from the agency. Each professional held an iPad with an application called SkyView®. When the iPad was held to the starry sky, SkyView magnified and identified the stars and constellations.

Loretta's sighted partner held the iPad in front of her eyes. With the tiny bit of sight Loretta had and the help of the screen's magnification, she suddenly gasped. "Tonight I saw God!"

Loretta was not the only one moved by this experience. After the visually impaired clients went home, the agency staff sat on the porch and discussed the experience during what amounted to a group therapy session.

Sharon began to cry, for the first time, about the experience of blindness.

"I cried so hard I had to lie down on the floor," she said. "But it wasn't about me. It was about the other people."

At that point Sharon knew that bringing adaptive technology to those with sight and hearing challenges was her life's mission.

RESOURCES SUMMARY

Resources are a source of supply, support, information, or expertise. In our car analogy, resources are the fuel that powers our vehicle. Resources may be physical (food, shelter, clothing), financial (paycheck, savings), social (emotional support, access to other resources), or internal (our own personal attributes and experience). Resources are specific to each individual's life experience and situation, and sometimes perception is stronger than reality — for good or bad.

After we've assessed our Experience and Assumptions, we can look at Resources more methodically:

❖ What resources do I *have*?
❖ What resources do I *need*?
❖ What resources do I need to *learn to live without*?

To help someone in crisis, we can observe and offer what's needed, ask what's needed, and offer what resources we have, even if we're not quite sure how they fit into the picture.

Conclusion

Thirty-seven years. From my first miscarriage on October 9, 1977, to November 27, 2014, it was thirty-seven years. During those years I experienced births and deaths, marriages and divorces, jobs that flourished and jobs that foundered.

I learned from wise people how to drive through life's rutted roads, sometimes getting stuck, but eventually moving forward. I learned from everything you have read in this book.

The rutted roads of my life merged into a smoother highway on Thanksgiving Day 2014. What happened that day?

Gathered around the table were my daughters, my son-in-law, his parents, sister, and niece, my first husband and his wife, my ninety-one-year-old mother, and my four-month-old grandson. Generations, cultures, marital connections past and present—none of those societal divisions mattered. In spite of past traumas, hurts, or misunderstandings, in spite of geographic distance, nothing mattered but bringing together this disparate yet loving group around a holiday and a baby.

But it did not happen by chance.

I hosted the gathering, and everyone contributed food and hands-on help to create the type of holiday *comfort* depicted in a Norman Rockwell painting.

Months of painstaking planning gave us some *control* over a chaotic time, even when the niece required a brief trip to the ER on Thanksgiving morning.

By reaching deep into the *community* of an extended family linked by bonds stronger than traditional categories, old wounds were healed.

A mutual *connection* to faith, tradition, and shared history allowed each of us to create new memories.

After *experiencing* years of separation, we found ways to overcome geographic and emotional distances.

One overriding *assumption* was certain: we wanted to be together and we wanted to enjoy the baby.

Each person found the *resources* necessary, sometimes creatively, to participate in this historic, healing holiday.

The powerful assumption that gripped my husband and me in 1977 was culminating thirty-seven years later. In spite of circumstances we could not foresee, we *were* supposed to be parents. Our pathways to resilience parted, but we each found what we needed, and so did our family.

Whatever shocks you encounter, I hope that you too will find what you need as you travel the road from reaction to resilience.

To your resilient best,

Becky

Acknowledgements

Rather than saving the best for last, I want to thank my family first. Laurie and Anna, my wise and forgiving daughters, grew up with a sometimes chaotic schedule due to my crisis-driven work. Even as children, they instinctively laughed and cried at the right times over the stories I could share. They were polite to scores of funeral directors, social workers, nurses, and all of my crisis intervention colleagues — not a fun crowd for teenagers. Most of all, like my steadfast mother, Fran, they lovingly badgered me with one injunction: Tell the stories.

That charge might have remained unfulfilled had it not been for my collaborator and editor, Karin Wiberg. She gently drew out the raw information, then worked with me to shape it and put it on the page in a way readers would understand and embrace. Karin has an amazing talent for seeing the big picture and fitting the puzzle pieces together, while looking at the details to make sure each word does its job. She pushed and challenged me to create the best book possible. On top of all that she held my hand through the entire creative process, including those scary parts in the middle where a project can feel overwhelming and confidence can falter. I am forever grateful.

Book cover designer Abby Greene and illustrator Shannon Baur similarly molded my thoughts into visuals that created clarity combined with subtlety. Both of them listened intently, modified concepts frequently, and focused on images meaningful for the reader. Plus, they are both very thoughtful women.

I am deeply indebted to the folks who allowed us into private corners of their lives, sharing the unvarnished versions of their crises and turning points. In order of appearance in the book, they are: Laurie Ray, Trey Owen and his parents, Rob and Norma Owen, Annie Rodriguez Freed, Larry Lytle, Rachelle Friedman Chapman, Jim Bankston, and Sharon Giovinazzo. In addition, thank you to the many people from whose stories I've created composite characters and examples.

If it takes a village to raise a child, it takes a city to create a book. Thank you, thank you to this community of generous volunteers, each of whom I am privileged to call a friend. Because of that, I will list your names in alphabetical order within your category of service to this project.

Beta readers: Mercedes Auger, Lee Heinrich, Bill Howe, Tonya McCoy, Stephanie McDilda, Norma Owen, Lisa Pineiro, CJ Scarlet, and Jessica White.

Proof readers: Marcia Adelberg, Mercedes Auger, Lee Heinrich, and Mary Wiberg.

Professional insights and ongoing emotional support: Lana Calloway, Mary Cantando, Chris Cimino, Ann Jagger, Allegra Jordan, Brenda Larson, Terry Lawyer, Carena Lemons, Lee Anne McClymont, Ahana Muth, Christine Peterson, Kevin Snyder, Mimi Soule, and Nannette Stangle-Castor.

I dare not conclude this list without thanking the Write Rite Group at the City Club Raleigh who patiently listened to my updates, offered wise suggestions, and tolerated my excuses for why I had not started writing my book...until one member, Karin Wiberg, caught me standing alone, looked me straight in the eye, and softly said, "Becky, exactly how far along are you with writing that book?"

I offer my heartfelt appreciation to every person on these pages, and undoubtedly some wonderful people whom I have accidentally overlooked.

Appendices

Appendix A: Detailed Table of Contents
Appendix B: Chapter Summaries
Appendix C: Chapter Notes and References

Appendix A:
Detailed Table of Contents

Appendix B:
Chapter Summaries

COMFORT

Comfort is a state of physical or emotional ease. On our Vehicle of Life it is one of the tires that (when inflated) provides stability and a smooth ride. Comfort allows us some separation from crisis, at least for a moment, so that we can rest and refocus before continuing.

What brings us each comfort is personal and depends on our individual life experiences. We may find comfort in physical things, in emotional bonds, or in particular activities. Rituals and traditions are two major sources of comfort in crisis, as they reinforce normalcy, connection, and continuity.

In our culture, we often have trouble talking about comfort, sometimes from a fear of appearing narcissistic or self-indulgent. When helping others in crisis, we may need to help them name the pain before they can identify what they need for comfort. Ask questions, pay attention to verbal and physical cues, and offer new ideas when you have permission. Recognize also the need to help family members and professional personnel align their actions with the needs and wants of the person in crisis.

CONTROL

Control is the power to make decisions about how something is managed or done, or the ability to direct the actions of someone or something. While we sometimes have a cultural attitude that people who seek control are "control freaks," in reality Control offers stability and a sense of safety, especially in crisis. Even a small addition of air to this tire on our Vehicle of Life can help us regain normalcy.

Like Comfort, Control is personal, based on our own life experiences. To regain control in a crisis, it helps to reconstitute daily habits, identify small things to control, break big things into small pieces, ignore things that can be ignored, and ask for and accept help.

When helping others in crisis, as with Comfort, remember the Platinum Rule ("Do unto other as *they* want to be done unto"). Understand the other person's pre-crisis "normal," and model normalcy for them. Offer practical help and space to gain perspective. Don't offer platitudes, comparisons, or ambiguous "help." Don't do nothing, and don't smother. Remember, Control is personal. Find out what the person in crisis needs to feel more safe and stable.

COMMUNITY

Community at its core is a unified body of individuals. It may be based on geography or interest. It may be family, friends, or neighbors. However defined, community possesses the practical and emotional support to help us move through a crisis toward stability.

While we depend on our community in crisis, we may have to politely manage or coordinate it to avoid overwhelm and use it most effectively. It's OK to vary our community and to keep parts of our community at arm's length when in crisis. If we find ourselves avoiding members of the community or trying to "protect" them, it may be wise to talk with a "safe stranger." A safe stranger is a trusted confidant during a period of crisis, who then typically exits our life so we can conclude one chapter and move on to the next.

Sometimes our community can fail us in crisis, whether due to fatigue, lack of size and skills, or oversight. Then we must decide if we have the fortitude to let the failure go, if we lovingly release that part of our community, or if we set aside the failure temporarily and look at it again later.

Even with the possibility of uplifting support or crushing disappointment, a community still offers the greatest potential for stabilizing us when we hit one of life's potholes. A community can provide the resources, the person-power, and the encouragement to pump up that third tire of our Vehicle of Life. In return, we can show them how to keep on driving, even when the road is bumpy.

CONNECTION

Connection is that thing that touches our spirit. It is that thing that comforts, uplifts, sustains, and enriches us. In a nutshell, we want to put our lives in context so we understand our own role and importance in the universe and know that we are contributing to an ongoing good.

Connection is personal. We may find it in any number of ways: philanthropy, music, art, literature, sports, nature, heritage, religion, spirituality, humor. As with Comfort, Connection may come through rituals and traditions. In crisis, Connection brings us purpose, meaning, and strength to carry on in the face of difficulties.

Our connection to religion in particular can be affected by crisis. We may find ourselves strengthening our connection, having our religious practices disrupted, losing our connection, or returning to our religious roots after being away. Religious or not, any form of connection is subject to shifts due to a crisis.

Expanding our own connections in daily life and encouraging connection for others inflates that tire on our Vehicle of Life, better positioning us to move through crises when they hit. As with the other Cs, remember Connection is personal; ask questions and listen closely to find the right connection for the person in crisis.

EXPERIENCE

Experience encompasses the conscious events that make up an individual life and the skill or knowledge obtained by doing something. In our car metaphor, experience is the frame of the car. It contains us, protects us, and offers a window to look through.

Whether our crisis is a difficulty, an acute crisis, a chronic crisis, or a life-altering change, we can use a series of questions to help us leverage past experience:

❖ Have I experienced **this situation** before? If so, what can I apply from that experience?

❖ Have I experienced **anything like this** before? If so, what can I apply from that experience?

❖ Is there anyone in my **inner circle** or **outer circle** that has had this experience or one like it before? If so, what can they help me learn about it?

❖ What else do I know that can help **mitigate the problem** even if I can't solve it?

In managing our crisis experience, we may find it useful to gather information, keep a journal, have someone else take notes for us, and talk to a safe stranger.

When helping someone else manage a crisis experience, it is important to keep in mind our own role as inner or outer circle and to act appropriately in that role. Common pitfalls include trying to solve someone else's problem or make someone else's decision, not asking for help, avoiding problems that surface, pulling away, and mistaking our role and whose needs we're trying to meet. To make sure we best meet the needs of the person in crisis, it helps to ask "When, where, and how can I be of most help?"

ASSUMPTIONS

Assumptions are those things we take for granted as true. We may also call them perceptions, beliefs, or understandings.

They may or may not be factually true, but they underpin our worldview and our choices. In our car metaphor, assumptions are the steering or guidance system.

The assumptions we hold about ourselves, about others, and about the world around us come from many sources: family, friends, faith, media, schools, community. Our assumptions shape our actions. If we can learn to shape our assumptions, they can more effectively serve us.

In crisis our goal is to use the power of our assumptions in an authentic, positive way to support and strengthen us as we move through a crisis toward resilience. We can use a methodical process:

1. Identify our assumptions related to this situation or crisis
2. Focus on two or three empowering authentic assumptions
3. Adapt or reframe authentic assumptions (positive or negative) to maintain authentic positive support
4. Throw away or replace assumptions that are getting in our way
5. Put some assumptions aside to look at again later

When we walk alongside those in crisis, our role is to help them assess and use their own assumptions by offering truth with kindness and holding open the door of possibility, while not letting our own assumptions get in the way.

RESOURCES

Resources are a source of supply, support, information, or expertise. In our car analogy, resources are the fuel that powers our vehicle. Resources may be physical (food, shelter, clothing), financial (paycheck, savings), social (emotional support, access to other resources), or internal (our own personal attributes and experience). Resources are specific to each individual's life experience and situation, and sometimes perception is stronger than reality—for good or bad.

After we've assessed our Experience and Assumptions, we can look at Resources more methodically:

- ❖ What resources do I *have*?
- ❖ What resources do I *need*?
- ❖ What resources do I need to *learn to live without*?

To help someone in crisis, we can observe and offer what's needed, ask what's needed, and offer what resources we have, even if we're not quite sure how they fit into the picture.

Appendix C:
Chapter Notes and References

Overview
- Merriam-Webster's free online dictionary has been used for definitions throughout this book.
- *The Human Dimensions of Resilience*, by Terri I. Sivilli and Thaddeus W.W. Pace, is a paper published by The Garrison Institute, Inc., 2014. It can be found at https://www.garrisoninstitute.org/transforming-trauma/contemplative-based-resilience-training.

Comfort
- There are multiple medical instruments for assessing pain. A common one is the Numeric Rating Scale (NRS-11), which asks patients to rate their pain on a scale of 0 to 10:
    - 0 = No pain
    - 1 to 3 = Mild pain
    - 4 to 6 = Moderate pain
    - 7 to 10 = Severe pain
- A twelve-step program is a set of guiding principles designed to address problems such as alcoholism, drug addiction, and other compulsive behaviors. The first of the twelve steps is admission of a problem, e.g., being powerless over alcohol. Alcoholics Anonymous was the first twelve-step program. Different people find different approaches to addiction-recovery helpful. This reference should not be construed as an endorsement of any individual program.

Control
- Joan Didion's book *The Year of Magical Thinking* (Knopf, 2005) chronicles the period after her husband of forty years died while her daughter also lay in a coma. She describes how grief took her to a state of "magical thinking." "We might expect that we will be prostrate, inconsolable, crazy with loss," she writes. "We do not expect to be literally crazy, cool customers who believe that their husband is about to return and need his shoes."
- The Platinum Rule comes from Dr. Tony Alessandra. For more information, visit his website at www.alessandra.com.

Community
- According to Facebook's website (http://newsroom.fb.com/company-info/), it had 1.44 billion monthly active users as of March 31, 2015.
- CaringBridge (www.caringbridge.org) is a web service designed to allow people in crisis (often medical in nature) to share updates with friends and family, receive messages from them, and coordinate care. Similar sites include CarePages.com and PostHope.org. Before you

sign up for these types of sites, I recommend you research their capabilities and privacy features to make sure they meet your needs.

* Betty Ford's breast cancer quote came from the article "Breast Cancer: Fear and Facts" in *Time* magazine, November 4, 1974.
* The quote about Betty Ford's "put[ting] a face on alcoholism as a disease" came from Dessa Bergen-Cico, assistant professor of Public Health and Addiction Studies at Syracuse University, in an ABC News story following Betty Ford's death July 8, 2011. The article can be found at http://abcnews.go.com/Health/betty-ford-pioneer-redefined-role-lady-put-face/story?id=14036838.

Connection

* Statistics on religion come from the Pew Research Center. The report "America's Changing Religious Landscape," published May 12, 2015, has data through 2014 and can be found at http://www.pewforum.org/2015/05/12/americas-changing-religious-landscape/.

A summary of Pew's U.S. religious affiliation data from 2014:

Christian		70.6%
Protestant	46.5	
Catholic	20.8	
Other	3.3	
Non-Christian faiths		5.9
Unaffiliated		22.8
Atheist	3.1	
Agnostic	4.0	
Nothing in particular	15.8	
Don't know/refused		0.6
Total		100.0%

* An earlier Pew report, "'Nones' on the Rise," published October 9, 2012, has data through 2012 and can be found at http://www.pewforum.org/2012/10/09/nones-on-the-rise/.

Experience

* Memory and Therapy – Dr. Sandra Bond Chapman, PhD, is Founder and Chief Director of the Center for BrainHealth at the University of Texas at Dallas. She was quoted in the *Women's Health* article "Why Having a Selective Memory Can Be a Very Good Thing," which can be found online at http://www.womenshealthmag.com/life/letting-bad-memories-go. You can read more about Dr. Chapman and her work at http://www.brainhealth.utdallas.edu/.
* According to the National Breast Cancer Foundation, Inc., one in eight women (in the U.S.) will be diagnosed with breast cancer in their lifetime (http://www.nationalbreastcancer.org/breast-cancer-facts).
* An Employee Assistance Program (EAP) is an employee benefit program offered by many employers. It provides help with personal

problems that may affect employees' job performance, health and well-being. Assistance typically includes short-term counseling or referrals to needed resources.

Assumptions

- Rachelle Chapman's book about her paralysis experience is titled *The Promise: A Tragic Accident, a Paralyzed Bride, and the Power of Love, Loyalty, and Friendship* (Skirt!, 2014).
- Post-traumatic growth (PTG) is positive change experienced as a result of the struggle with a major life crisis or a traumatic event. Some of the principle investigators on this topic are from the University of North Carolina at Charlotte, and include Lawrence G. Calhoun, Richard G. Tedeschi, Arnie Cann, and Amy Canevello. For more about research on PTG, visit https://ptgi.uncc.edu/.
- Steven Covey's business and self-help book *The 7 Habits of Highly Effective People: Powerful Lessons in Personal Change* was first published in 1989 (Free Press). The 7 Habits include: 1) Be proactive, 2) Begin with the end in mind, 3) Put first things first, 4) Think win-win, 5) Seek first to understand, then to be understood, 6) Synergize, and 7) Sharpen the saw.

Resources

- Abraham Maslow presented his Hierarchy of Needs in 1943 in a paper titled "A Theory of Human Motivation." It is typically represented as a five-level pyramid with the more basic needs at the bottom. From bottom to top, the levels are: Physiological needs (food, clothing, shelter), Safety needs (personal, financial, etc.), Love and Belonging needs (friendship, intimacy, family), Esteem needs (self-respect, respect from others), and Self-actualization needs (realization of potential). Much information, including critique of the model, can be found online.
- SMART Recovery is another support method for dealing with addictions. SMART stands for Self-Management and Recovery Training. SMART Recovery is a 4-point program that uses science-based methods. More information can be found at: http://www.smartrecovery.org/. Different people find different approaches to addiction-recovery helpful. This reference should not be construed as an endorsement of any individual program.
- Read Adrianne Haslet-Davis's story at http://blog.ted.com/more-on-adrianne-haslet-davis-journey-to-dance-again-in-a-cnn-special-report/.

21846255R00145

Made in the USA
Middletown, DE
13 July 2015